Zoodles

spiralizer
cookbook

SONNET LAUBERTH

Zoodles

spiralizer cookbook

A Vegetable Noodle &
Pasta Cookbook

Photographs by Shannon Douglas

ROCKRIDGE
PRESS

This book is dedicated to my mother,

who taught me that the
most important moments in life
happen in the kitchen.

For general information on our other products and services or to obtain technical support, please contact our Customer Care Department within the United States at (866) 744–2665, or outside the United States at (510) 253–0500.

Rockridge Press publishes its books in a variety of electronic and print formats. Some content that appears in print may not be available in electronic books, and vice versa.

TRADEMARKS: Rockridge Press and the Rockridge Press logo are trademarks or registered trademarks of Callisto Media Inc. and/or its affiliates, in the United States and other countries, and may not be used without written permission. All other trademarks are the property of their respective owners. Rockridge Press is not associated with any product or vendor mentioned in this book.

ISBN: Print 978-1-62315-776-0 | eBook 978-1-62315-777-7

Contents

Introduction

I BELIEVE OUR HEALTH is the foundation for living a happy life, and the best thing we can do for ourselves is to take care of our bodies. I also believe that food is meant to be enjoyed, and if we're not eating delicious food, then *what's the point?*

Throughout my life I've struggled with multiple health challenges, so I understand firsthand the importance of eating fresh, healthy food. However, I'm also realistic, and I know how hard it can be to eat healthfully in our busy, fast-paced world.

Back in 2010, I began writing my food blog, *In Sonnet's Kitchen*, with the hope that sharing tasty, healthy recipes would inspire others to realize that healthy eating doesn't have to be boring or complicated. This is exactly why I love spiralizing!

I bought my first spiralizer in 2008 when I was working at a vegan cafe in Seattle. In those days, no one was talking about going grain-free or spiralizing, but I instantly fell in love with the little gadget because it was easy; added a fun, creative flair to meals; and made it possible to sneak even more vegetables into a dish.

Throughout my career as a certified holistic health coach, food blogger, and cooking instructor working with both children and adults, I've created a lot of spiralizing converts. Spiralizing is a wonderful way to enjoy healthier versions of your favorite comfort foods while getting more vegetables (and fruit!) into your diet. You'll be amazed at how this one simple change can affect the way you think about food and your overall health.

This book and the foods in it are a reflection of how I eat and the dishes I love to make. My diet is always evolving, based on the needs of my body and my lifestyle, and you'll see this reflected in the recipes. They include vegan/plant-based, vegetarian, and meat dishes (although these can be adapted to a vegan or vegetarian diet). All the recipes are gluten-free, dairy-free, and free of refined sugars and processed foods. All adhere to a Paleo diet.

My food philosophy is that eating a variety of fresh, seasonal vegetables and loading up your plate with whole foods never goes out of style. I hope this book inspires you to make appetizing meals that taste great while nourishing your body.

Now, let's get to spiralizing!

1

Noodle Around:
An Introduction to Spiralizing

Spiralizing is not only fun, but it will also change the way you think about food and cooking. A spiralizer is an inexpensive little gadget that cuts fresh vegetables into long, curvy strips—basically, faux noodles. This chapter will teach you all the basics you need to know: everything from what type of spiralizer to buy to tips and best practices for preparing your vegetable noodles!

The Healthy Noodle

Everyone loves pasta and noodles. But since most pastas are made from refined white flour, they're not the healthiest choice for everyday meals. This is where a spiralizer (also known as a spiral slicer) comes in.

Regardless of your specific health goals, food preferences, or dietary needs, spiralizing can help you:

* Remove processed foods from your diet while still enjoying tasty meals.

* Transition to a gluten-free or completely grain-free diet.

* Reduce your overall carbohydrate intake, while also incorporating healthier sources of carbohydrates (vegetables) instead of refined flour.

* Lose weight by making healthier versions of your favorite dishes.

* Eat more vegetables and fruit, which increases the overall nutrition in your diet by including vitamins, minerals, fiber, and phytochemicals (such as antioxidants) that you can only get from plants.

* Have more fun in the kitchen! With so many people eating convenience foods and take-out, somewhere along the way we lost the joy of cooking. Spiralizing is a great way to enjoy creating healthy meals from scratch.

* Cut down on prep time when cooking meals from scratch. The average pot of pasta takes around 12 minutes to cook (and that's not including the time it takes to boil the water), but most veggie noodles can be ready in as little as 3 to 5 minutes—or eaten raw, depending on the dish.

* Incorporate a wider array of vegetables into your diet. The most commonly eaten vegetable in the United States is potatoes, followed by tomatoes, corn, and lettuce. But there is so much more variety available. With spiralizing, you can enjoy more nutritional powerhouse veggies like broccoli, cabbage, bell peppers, kohlrabi, celeriac, and daikon radishes.

* Get the whole family involved in cooking and eating healthy together. When I was a food educator working with young children, it never failed that the best way to get a picky eater to try a new vegetable was to get them involved in preparing the food. Try this with your kids, a veggie-fearing significant other, or even yourself. You might be surprised at the results!

Making the Most of Your Spiralizer

Spiralizers have come a long way since I bought my first one, and now there are countless brands on the market. If you're new to spiralizing and don't have a spiralizer yet, it can be a bit intimidating to figure out which model to get. But don't worry, I'm here to help.

Spiralizers fall into two basic categories: hand-crank models and hourglass models. Let's take a look at both and break down their pros and cons, so you can decide which is the best model for you.

Food Cravings

Food cravings are normal and our body's way of communicating with us. They can be caused by a physical need, as well as our emotions, mental state, and environment. For example, have you ever noticed that you crave sugar when you're under stress or not getting enough sleep? Or maybe you tend to crave hearty, creamy dishes in the cold winter? Or perhaps you want juicy foods like sorbet or watermelon in the hot weather because you're dehydrated?

Many people feel guilty about having food cravings and believe they are signs of weakness. This couldn't be further from the truth. The key is to learn how to decode our cravings and work *with* our body instead of against it. One way I deal with food cravings is to replace the item with a healthier version, so try these substitutions and see how they work for you:

* Craving mac and cheese? Try Fettuccine with Rosemary Butternut Crème Sauce (page 46), Truffle Pasta with Kale and Roasted Cauliflower (page 49), or Smoky Mac and "Cheese" (page 32).

* Craving Fettuccine Alfredo? Try the spiralizer version (page 38) with rutabagas, cauliflower, and cashews, or Leek and Sage Crème Sauce over Pasta (page 48).

* Craving classic spaghetti? Try a veggie noodle take with Spaghetti with Beef Bolognese (page 42), Spaghetti with Meatballs (page 40), or Spaghetti with Mushroom Marinara (page 33).

* Craving takeout? Try Chicken and Veggie Chow Mein (page 70), Sweet Potato Yakisoba (page 62), or Weekend Pad Thai with Chicken (page 66).

I recommend the hand-crank models for users of all levels. The hand-crank models usually cost a little more, and they take up more space in the kitchen, but they also produce the best noodles and give you the most variety of noodle shapes. Each brand is slightly different, but all of them come with multiple blades (generally three or four), so you can make a variety of pasta shapes and sizes.

Popular hand-crank brands include:

* Paderno World Cuisine Tri-Blade Spiral Vegetable Slicer
* The Inspiralizer
* Spiralizer Tri-Blade Vegetable Spiral Slicer
* WonderVeg Tri Blade Spiral Slicer

Pros and Cons

The hand-crank model is going to give you the most versatility, because it will spiralize any vegetable that can be spiralized. This includes larger vegetables like butternut squash, jicama, and sweet potatoes, which you would have to precut to be able to spiralize with the hourglass model.

Because this type of spiralizer has suction cups to keep it securely on the counter, you have more control so you can even spiralize tough vegetables (such as celeriac) without worrying about slicing your finger on the blade.

The hand-crank models remove the core of the vegetable as you spiralize, which is particularly helpful for zucchini, since their centers contain the most moisture and seeds. Removing the core results in less-watery zoodles compared to the hourglass models.

Hand-crank models are very quick and easy to use. You can create veggie noodles for an entire dish in under 2 minutes!

The Inspiralizer model in particular has a few unique features that make it a great choice. I especially like that you can change the blades by turning a handle (instead of having to push or pull the blades in and out individually), and there's also a safety cover that protects your fingers from the blades when it's not in use.

Of course, there are some cons as well. Hand-crank models need to be handwashed. You'll need to clean all the nooks and crannies with a small dishwashing or vegetable brush. And most hand-crank models are about the size of a medium toaster, so they take up more storage space in the kitchen than the hourglass models. Hand-crank models can also cost more than the hourglass models; most range from $25 to $50.

Usage and Safety

To use a hand-crank model, start by installing the selected blade, depending on the type of pasta desired. (In every recipe, I'll tell you exactly which blade you need.) Next, prepare your vegetable by slicing off the ends and peeling it, if necessary. Center the vegetable on the cylindrical piece of the blade then push the spikes of the handle into the other side of the vegetable, so it is secure in the machine. Turn the handle clockwise to begin spiralizing.

Since spiralizers have sharp blades (and no one likes emergency trips to the doctor), there are some safety considerations to keep in mind, even with a hand-crank model.

* Children should never use a spiralizer without adult supervision.

* If your model has separate blade attachments, when changing blades be sure to hold the blade by the top plastic piece and pull upward, keeping your fingers away from the actual—very sharp—blade.

* Be extremely careful where you put your fingers when washing the blades. Likewise, don't leave them under a pile of other washed dishes in the dish drainer, where someone could accidentally touch the sharp edges.

* Vegetables (especially harder vegetables like sweet potatoes) can sometimes get stuck in the blade. Use a dishwashing or vegetable brush to remove any vegetables that may get stuck, and be sure the blade is clean for the next use.

* Sometimes the core of the vegetable can get stuck in the blade. Be sure to use a thin cylindrical object, like a butter knife or a chopstick (not a finger!), to help pop the vegetable out of the blade.

HOURGLASS MODELS

The hourglass models work best with soft produce that is already cylindrical and thin, such as zucchini and cucumbers. However, with a little extra prep you can spiralize larger produce. This model is good as a starter, especially if you're curious to try spiralizing but don't want to spend a lot of money or take up extra room in your kitchen. If you find you love it and want to do more, you can always get a hand-crank model later.

Popular hourglass brands include:

* Vegetti
* Brieftons Spiral Slicer
* SpiraLife
* Kitchen Active Spiralizer Spiral Slicer

Pros and Cons

Hourglass models are small and take up very little storage space. They're inexpensive too—most range from $10 to $20. They're very simple to use, and are dishwasher safe. Most hourglass models come with two blade sizes so you still get some variety, although less than with a hand-crank model.

Waste Not

One of the many benefits of cooking at home is that preparing your own meals helps you save money. To save even more, plus live in a more sustainable way by not being wasteful, be sure to use all the vegetable scraps created by your spiralizer. Try juicing zucchini scraps, blending cucumber scraps into green smoothies, using parsnip scraps in soups, puréeing daikon radish scraps in homemade hummus, or using sweet potato scraps in a breakfast scramble.

You can also save veggie scraps in a bag in your freezer, and when the bag is full, boil them to make your own vegetable broth. This works particularly well with scraps of root vegetables (such as carrots, parsnips, and sweet potatoes) and aromatics (such as onions, garlic, leeks, and shallots).

Cruciferous vegetable scraps (such as broccoli, cabbage, and kohlrabi) will add a sour flavor to your broth, but they can be added fresh to any soup or stew you have bubbling on the stove, or tossed raw into a salad. Also, if you don't want your broth to be red, be sure to leave red beets out of the mix.

There are some disadvantages, though. If you are spiralizing large vegetables (such as butternut squash or jicama), you will have to precut them so they can fit into the opening. Vegetables that will not hold together in smaller chunks, such as cabbage and onions, just won't work with an hourglass model.

Hourglass models also do not remove the core of the vegetable, so if you are spiralizing a vegetable with a high water content like zucchini, the noodles can be very watery and may break apart easily. Hard vegetables tend to get stuck easily, as well, so you might still have to hand-clean the spiral cutter to remove any pieces of leftover veggies before sticking it in the dishwasher. (Many models come with a brush for exactly this reason.)

Hourglass models take a bit of time and manpower, because you're hand-turning the vegetable pieces through the machine. If you're trying to make dinner for your whole family, this might be challenging.

Usage and Safety

Hourglass models work in a way similar to a handheld pencil sharpener. Prepare your vegetable by slicing off the ends and peeling it, if necessary. If it's not shaped like a zucchini or a carrot, cut it into pieces that will fit through the center of the hourglass. Some hourglass models do come with a separate handle that you stick the vegetable on and use to crank it through, so your finger can't touch the blades. Center the vegetable inside the spiralizer or on the spikes of the handle, depending on the model. Turn your hand clockwise while pushing the vegetable into the spiralizer.

Safety is a big concern for hourglass models. Since you are using your hand to turn the vegetable and crank it through the blade, it could slice your finger. Even though some come with a handle, I would never feel comfortable letting a child (or distracted adult for that matter) use an hourglass model. Here are some things to keep in mind:

* Be sure to keep fingers away from the blades when pushing the vegetable through.

* If the vegetable becomes stuck, use a thin cylindrical object, like a butter knife or a chopstick (not a finger!), to remove the vegetable.

* If you do handwash your hourglass model, be very careful where you put your fingers when washing the inside, because the blades are exposed. Likewise, don't leave it beneath a pile of unwashed dishes in the sink or washed dishes in the rack, where someone might accidentally touch the sharp edges.

Noodle Varieties

One satisfying thing about spiralizing is that you can make a recipe feel different just by switching the type of noodles. The type and model of spiralizer you own will determine the number of blades you have and the types of noodles you can create. Hand-crank models offer the most variety, since they generally come with three or four blades. Hourglass models typically have two blades—usually spaghetti and fettuccine.

Every recipe will suggest a blade, depending on the type of noodle that works best. However, if you don't have the blade suggested, feel free to use the basic spaghetti blade, or whichever blade you have available. It will still taste delicious.

Let's look at the different blades and the type of noodle each blade will create.

* **Fettuccine blade:** This blade creates thicker noodles, similar to fettuccine or linguine. It has the largest triangles on it, or, if you're using the hourglass model, use the side with the blades farthest apart.

* **Spaghetti blade:** This blade creates noodles similar to spaghetti or ramen. It has smaller triangles on it (compared to the fettuccine blade), or, if you're using the hourglass model, use the side with the blades closest together.

* **Ribbon blade:** This blade creates a thin ribbon noodle (similar to pappardelle), and is different from the other blades since it is flat and does not have any triangles on the cutting surface. The hourglass model does not have this blade, so if you are preparing a recipe that calls for the ribbon blade, use the side with the blades farthest apart.

* **Angel Hair Blade:** Some hand-crank models come with a fourth blade that creates thin noodles similar to angel hair pasta. This blade will have the smallest triangles on it. Since not every model of spiralizer comes with this option, it is not specifically called for in any recipe. However, if you do have it, you can use it in place of the spaghetti blade for any of the recipes.

Spiral-Friendly Produce

For the first couple of years that I owned a spiralizer, I only spiralized zucchini. Although zoodles are absolutely fabulous, there's so much more you can do with your spiralizer! This section will give you some helpful tips so you can get more vegetables and more variety into your diet.

SPIRALIZE IT

When you look at a spiralizer, even a hand-crank one, you see that the produce has to fit on a holder and have enough density to hold together as it is cut. There are five key qualities that make a fruit or vegetable "spiralizer-worthy."

* **Length:** Ideally the fruit or vegetable should be at least 1½ to 2 inches long. Otherwise you won't get many noodles and there will be a lot of vegetable scraps left over.

* **Width:** To avoid half-moon or short noodle pieces, your fruit or vegetable should be at least 1½ inches wide.

* **Firmness:** A fruit or vegetable needs to be firm, or it will be shredded when it is pushed through the blade.

* **No pits:** Any fruit with a tough pit can't go through the spiralizer blade. (In addition, if it has a pit, the fruit is most likely too soft to spiralize.)

* **Seedless:** Ideally, your fruit or vegetable does not contain hard or inedible seeds, although there are a few exceptions to this rule:
  * Even though butternut squash has hard seeds, by cutting off the bulbous end and only using the upper part of the fruit, it can be spiralized.
  * Cantaloupe can also be spiralized by removing the hard rind, spiralizing the fruit, and then when you reach the middle and see seeds coming through the spiralizer, scoop them out and resume spiralizing.

* Bell pepper can actually be spiralized even though it has a hollow middle with seeds. Simply remove the stem, spiralize the bell pepper (I recommend the ribbon blade) and then after spiralizing, remove and compost the seeds and ribs.

Putting the "Z" in Zoodles

Zucchini is definitely one of the most popular vegetables to spiralize, since it's low in carbohydrates, readily available, familiar, and works well in a variety of recipes. Here are a few tips to help you get the most from your zucchini pasta:

* Zucchini has a thin skin and does not need to be peeled before spiralizing. I like to leave the skin on to get the full nutritional benefits, but you can peel it if you'd like the zoodles to look more like traditional pasta (without patches of green).

* Zucchini pasta can be boiled or sautéed in a pan, and due to its high water content it will cook quickly (2 to 3 minutes, on average).

* If you haven't noticed already, the one downfall of zucchini pasta is that it gets watery after cooking. The best way to combat this is to cook the zoodles and sauce separately, then drain the zoodles before pouring the sauce on top. If you're in a hurry or don't want to dirty a colander, use tongs to pull the zoodles out of the pan and let the liquid drain before adding them to your dish.

* Zucchini pasta should never be frozen. I learned the hard way when I defrosted some and it turned into a pile of mush. Instead, if you're trying to get ahead on meal prep and want to store extra zoodles, keep raw zoodles in the refrigerator in an airtight glass container (to avoid the BPA in plastic), and they will keep for up to 5 days. Then cook them at the last minute for any recipe of your choice.

* If your spiralizer is creating half-moon pieces or short zoodles, be sure the zucchini is centered on the spiralizer.

* If your zucchini is very crooked (as some seasonal zucchini may be), try cutting it in half so you have two straighter pieces. This will help keep it better centered on the spiralizer and will yield longer zoodles.

Recipe Ideas for Your Produce

PRODUCE	HOW TO PREPARE	RECIPE
Apple	Remove the stem	Light and Crunchy Kohlrabi Slaw (page 84)
Beet	Raw: Peel and cut off the ends Cooked: Roast or boil the beet first, remove the skin, and spiralize	Pasta with Lemon-Crème Sauce and Salmon (page 52)
Bell Pepper	Remove the stem and shake out the seeds after you spiralize	Bread-Free BLT with Chipotle Ranch Dressing (page 101)
Broccoli stem	Peel and cut off the florets	Red Cabbage and Broccoli Slaw with Salmon and Orange-Sesame Dressing (page 94)
Butternut Squash	Cut off the bulbous end, peel the rest, and cut in half	Warm Winter Squash with Tangy Dressing (page 90)
Cabbage	Remove the outer layers and cut the bottom layer flat; if the cabbage is particularly large, cut it in half	Mongolian Beef over Cabbage (page 72)
Carrot	Peel and cut off the ends	Teriyaki Chicken with Carrot and Cabbage Slaw (page 63)
Celeriac	Peel and cut off the ends	Coconut-Lime Broccoli Stir-Fry (page 74)
Cucumber	Cut off the ends; use a paper towel to soak up extra moisture before adding to a dish	Arugula and Herb Greek Salad (page 87)
Daikon Radish	Peel and cut off the ends	Thai Lettuce Wraps with Pork (page 64)

PRODUCE	HOW TO PREPARE	RECIPE
Jicama	Peel and cut off the ends	Kale and Lime Caesar (page 92)
Kohlrabi	Peel and cut off the ends	Light and Crunchy Kohlrabi Slaw (page 84)
Onion	Remove the outer layers and cut off the ends	Avocado and Tuna Salad (page 93)
Parsnip	Peel and cut off the ends	Green Bean Casserole with a Twist (page 35)
Pear	Cut off the ends	Fall Harvest Salad with Toasted Pecans (page 89)
Potato (white)	Peel and cut off the ends	Lightened-Up Potato Salad (substitute white potatoes for sweet potatoes) (page 86)
Rutabaga	Peel and cut off the ends	Fettuccine Alfredo (page 38)
Summer Squash	Cut off the ends	Cacio e Pepe with Lemon and Arugula (page 34)
Sweet Potato	Peel and cut off the ends	Weekend Pad Thai with Chicken (page 66)
Turnip	Peel and cut off the ends	Pasta with Mushroom Sauce (page 51)
Zucchini	Cut off the ends	Spaghetti with Beef Bolognese (page 42)

Counting Carbs

One of the top benefits of eating vegetable noodles instead of wheat pasta is that you can decrease your overall carbohydrate intake and reduce or remove processed flours from your diet. For example, 1 cup of spaghetti has 43 grams of carbohydrates; if you consider the fact that most people probably eat 2 cups of pasta at a meal, this means you're consuming around 86 grams of carbohydrates in one meal. If you compare this with vegetable noodles, 2 cups of zucchini noodles contains only 7 grams of carbohydrates!

Our bodies do need a certain amount of carbohydrates to function properly, especially if you are active and engage in intense workouts. But what I love about spiralizing is that it gives you the chance to get your carbohydrates from vegetables and whole foods, like sweet potatoes or root vegetables, instead. Plus, if you struggle with blood sugar crashes from eating large amounts of carbohydrates, replacing wheat pasta and noodles with spiralized vegetables will help keep your blood sugar stable, which can also reduce sugar cravings and aid in overall weight loss.

DON'T SPIRALIZE IT

Unfortunately, there are a few fruits and veggies that don't make the cut when it comes to spiralizing. Vegetables that do not have the desired width, such as celery, asparagus, and green beans, cannot be spiralized. Vegetables and fruits that are too soft and/or juicy will also not work; a few examples are bananas, watermelon, pineapple, and tomatoes.

Eggplant appears as though you can spiralize it (it's similar enough to zucchini, right?), but it actually does not spiralize well due to its soft core. In addition, the florets of vegetables like broccoli and cauliflower cannot be spiralized, although broccoli stalks can, and you will see them in some of the recipes.

Going Organic

If you're reading this cookbook, I know you are interested in taking care of your body and health. One of the wonderful benefits of spiralizing is being able to include more fresh fruits and vegetables in your diet, so it's important to buy the healthiest produce possible. So let's talk about organic produce.

"Organic" means the produce is grown without the use of pesticides or chemical fertilizers and does not contain genetically modified organisms (GMOs). Here in the United States, the USDA controls the organic certification and labeling process, and a food can only be labeled "organic" if it contains a minimum of 95 percent organic ingredients.

Why is buying organic important for you and your family?

* Pesticides are poisons that are designed to kill living organisms; they are harmful to our bodies.

* Infants and young children are particularly vulnerable to the effects of these chemicals, since their immune systems and bodies are still developing.

* Buying organic and supporting organic farmers prevents chemicals from getting into our air, water, and food supply; promotes biodiversity; and protects future generations.

Before I go any further, let me ask you a question: If you haven't been buying organic produce up to this point, what is your greatest barrier?

When I was working as a holistic health coach, almost every time the topic of organic foods came up, no matter how much my clients agreed about the benefits of buying organic, they'd still choose conventional produce at the grocery store because of the cost. If you have a hard time justifying increasing your food budget, I hear you! As someone who spent many years working in the nonprofit industry, I understand tight budgets and how hard it can

be to shell out the extra money to buy organic produce. However, there are ways to buy organic and still work with a tight food budget.

Each year, the Environmental Working Group tests the pesticide residue in a wide variety of produce and updates their Dirty Dozen list (produce with the most pesticide residue) and their Clean Fifteen list (produce with the least pesticide residue). To avoid as many toxins as possible, my recommendation is to buy organic versions of the produce on the Dirty Dozen list. Since the items on the Clean Fifteen list contain relatively small amounts of pesticide residue, you can save a bit of cash by buying conventionally grown versions of these.

Both of these lists are available in Appendix B (page 124). For more information, visit the Non-GMO Project website (nongmoproject .org) or the Environmental Working Group's website (www.ewg.org).

Eating Locally and Seasonally

I believe in eating locally and seasonally as much as possible. Eating seasonally means eating foods that nature intended for our climate and at that particular time of the year. Our bodies naturally tend to crave certain foods at certain times of the year—for instance, a fresh, cooling salad in summer or a warm stew in winter. Eating seasonally connects us with the seasons and the weather. Eating locally means the food you are eating is grown nearby. If you are eating locally, this means that you are also eating seasonally because the food is being grown in your particular climate.

Why buy and eat locally and seasonally?

* Local foods travel a shorter distance to reach you, resulting in fresher food. And because the food is not shipped a long distance, both environmental pollution and our carbon footprint are reduced.

* Eating locally supports the local economy, supports local and smaller farmers who are farming sustainably, and creates community because you are more connected to the farmers who grow your food.

* Eating seasonally reduces food costs, because when we buy what is abundant and in season, the supply is greater and therefore the cost of the food is usually lower. This enables you to buy better quality items while stretching your food dollars.

* And—the best part—eating seasonally simply tastes better and fresher!

Along those lines, if you're cooking a dish that calls for zucchini and it's in the middle of winter, don't be afraid to substitute a root vegetable or butternut squash instead. One of the beautiful things about cooking at home is that you're in control of what you eat. So swap ingredients if they're out of season or just not grown locally. Or substitute vegetables you really love, if something else isn't a favorite.

Tips on Ingredients

Some of the ingredients in this cookbook may be new or unfamiliar, so I want to introduce them to you here, along with tips on how to use them.

ARROWROOT POWDER

Arrowroot is a starchy powder that comes from a tropical root. It is a wonderful alternative to cornstarch because it is also a natural thickening agent, but contains more nutrients than cornstarch. Arrowroot powder can be found at any health food store (in the baking section or bulk bins), some grocery stores, as well as online.

CASHEWS (RAW)

Depending on your dietary needs, you might be new to cooking without dairy. I use raw cashews to create creamy sauces, dressings, and mock "cheese," which replace dairy. I love cooking with cashews; they are loaded with healthy fats and proteins, and can be blended to create a cashew milk that's the perfect way to add creaminess to a dish.

If you don't have a high-performance blender (such as a Vitamix) or a good food processor, I recommend soaking the cashews before blending them into sauces and dressing. This will help soften them, so your sauce ends up smooth and creamy. Soak the cashews in a cup of water for at least 15 minutes then drain before blending.

Raw cashews are not roasted or salted, so they may not always be in the same aisle as the snacking nuts in your grocery store. Read the labels, and check your local health food store if you can't find them in the supermarket.

And if you are allergic to nuts or cannot eat cashews for some other reason, sunflower seeds are a wonderful alternative.

COCONUT AMINOS

Coconut aminos is a thin sauce made by aging the sap of the coconut tree. It contains naturally occurring amino acids and sea salt, so it adds a nice savory quality to recipes. Coconut aminos has a lighter, sweeter, and less salty taste than soy sauce or tamari, but it is often used as an alternative in Asian dishes.

I specify coconut aminos to meet the dietary needs of those who cannot have soy or gluten, or have concerns about sodium. You can find it in some supermarkets, most health food stores, and online.

COCONUT MILK (CANNED, FULL-FAT)

Coconut milk is an excellent dairy-free way to add creaminess to a curry, soup, or sauce. Every recipe that uses coconut milk calls for full-fat unsweetened canned coconut milk. This product is different from the coconut milk beverage that you find in the dairy section of the supermarket. Full-fat canned coconut milk is usually on the grocery shelves.

If you have concerns about the fat content of full-fat coconut milk, you can use part full-fat coconut milk and part water in the recipes, instead of buying light or low-fat coconut milk.

COOKING OILS

Different cooking oils have different smoke points, and you should pick your oil based on the cooking temperature of the recipe. This is important because when oil starts to smoke, it has been damaged and forms potentially carcinogenic substances. If you notice oil smoking in a pan, you should always discard it. If, for health reasons, you need to reduce the amount of fat in a recipe, you can omit the oil used for cooking and sauté the dish with broth or water instead.

Coconut oil is called for in the majority of recipes because it can be used with heat ranging from low to medium-high, making it

Fitting the Recipes Into your Diet

I've tried to make the recipes good for all types of diets and nutritional needs. None of them contain dairy, wheat, gluten, grains, refined sugars, legumes, soy, or shellfish. As a result, this book is also fabulous for anyone following a Paleo or primal diet, and many of the recipes work well for those on the Whole30 program.

For anyone who's vegetarian or vegan, feel free to omit any animal products and substitute vegetarian protein sources of your choice—including eggs if you're vegetarian, or organic sprouted tofu, tempeh, legumes, and so on if you're vegan. Recipes that are specifically vegetarian or vegan will be labeled as such, but many of these recipes can become vegetarian or vegan with a few easy substitutions.

Some of the recipes call for ingredients like kimchi or curry paste; depending on the brand, they may contain fish sauce. Be sure to check the labels if this is a concern for you. Some brands of curry paste may also contain gluten, so be sure to look for a brand that is specifically labeled gluten-free.

highly versatile for most cooking. It also adds a mild coconut flavor that can enhance a dish. **Safflower oil** is another great all-purpose oil due to its mild flavor and high smoke point, which also makes it a good oil to use for grilling. **Sesame oil** is a delicious oil typically used in Asian cuisine. It adds a nutty, sesame flavor to dishes, and can be used in medium-heat cooking.

Extra-virgin olive oil has a very low smoke point, so although it is famous for being a heart-healthy oil due to its monounsaturated fats, I recommend only using it uncooked. For this reason, you'll find olive oil used exclusively in raw salad dressings. Look for cold-pressed extra-virgin olive oil to get the maximum health benefits, and be sure to store the oil in a cool pantry or refrigerator to ensure it doesn't go rancid.

HONEY AND PURE MAPLE SYRUP

I prefer to rely on the natural sugars in fruits and vegetables as much as possible, but there are times in cooking (and in life) when you need a tad of extra sweetness. Some of the recipes call for honey or maple syrup, which I always prefer over white sugar since both of these natural sweeteners are less processed and gentler on the body. Honey is full of antioxidants and antibacterial properties. Pure maple syrup is made by boiling down the sap of sugar maple trees and is loaded with antioxidants and minerals. Just be sure the maple syrup is 100 percent pure (no maple-flavored corn syrup), and store maple syrup in the refrigerator to prevent mold.

NUTRITIONAL YEAST FLAKES

Nutritional yeast is a dietary supplement popular with vegans for its high vitamin B_{12} and protein content, and its delicious "cheesy" flavor. It's made from yeast that is washed and then dried with heat that deactivates it, so it doesn't froth like yeast for baking or brewing.

I use nutritional yeast because it works so well (and tastes so good) for dairy-free cooking. You can find it in health food stores, as well as online.

SEA SALT

Sea salt contains more minerals and is less processed than conventional table salt. Look for fine sea salt, which can be found in grocery stores or health food stores. Recipes call for a small amount of sea salt to enhance the flavors of a dish. However, if sodium is a concern, feel free to reduce or omit the salt entirely.

Kitchen Essentials

Regardless of your cooking ability and level of comfort in the kitchen, there are a few basic kitchen essentials you'll need to make the recipes.

CHEF'S KNIFE

A chef's knife is typically going to be the largest knife in your kitchen and the one you reach for most often when you're preparing food. If you're buying a big knife for the first time, look for one with a blade that is 8 to 10 inches long and that feels good and balanced in your hand. Since all of the recipes call for chopping or preparing vegetables in some form, you'll want to make sure your knife is sharp, so throw a small knife sharpener into your shopping bag. And, of course, practice good knife skills to keep yourself safe.

CUTTING BOARD

Along with a chef's knife, you'll also need a cutting board for prepping the recipes. I like to reserve one cutting board exclusively for preparing raw meats, and a separate board for chopping raw vegetables. This minimizes the risk of cross-contamination between raw meats and fresh vegetables (which may or may not be cooked), reducing your chances of spreading a foodborne illness.

DIGITAL THERMOMETER

As someone who for years has worked in kitchens and taught classes with a variety of chefs, I always use a thermometer when cooking meat and poultry, and you'll see that my recipes specify an internal temperature for animal proteins. This ensures that your food not only reaches a safe temperature (especially chicken, which must be cooked to at least 165°F), but also helps ensure that your food isn't overcooked. An instant-read or digital meat thermometer usually costs under $20.

DISHWASHING OR VEGETABLE BRUSH

One of the biggest complaints about using a spiralizer is that it's hard to clean. When I ask, people tell me that they have been trying to clean the blades and machine with a sponge. Although a sponge can be handy, I recommend buying a small dishwashing or vegetable brush for cleaning. This is the easiest and safest way to remove veggie noodles stuck to the blades, and ensures that your spiralizer is clean for the next use.

GLASS STORAGE CONTAINERS WITH LIDS

You may have leftovers, or you may decide to double up on a recipe so you have something for lunch the next day. Either way, a good set of storage containers will make this much easier. I like using glass, because you can reheat the food in a microwave directly in the container, and there aren't any concerns about BPA in plastic.

KITCHEN SHEARS

Kitchen shears are heavy-duty scissors—much stronger than your typical paper-cutting variety—that are perfect for kitchen tasks. They're fabulous for giving noodles a quick trim, which can be especially helpful for long zucchini noodles. I also love using kitchen shears to quickly cut up a bunch of fresh herbs to add extra flavor to dishes.

POTS AND PANS

By now, you may have heard about the dangers of nonstick pans. To avoid any chemicals leaching into the food, use a cast iron skillet, and 100 percent ceramic, cast iron, or stainless steel pots.

Cast iron is what your grandmother cooked with. It's heavy, but it's versatile and lasts forever. Cast iron should always be seasoned before using. This will keep noodles from sticking to the pan. Heat the oven to 350°F and apply a thin coat of coconut oil or cooking fat all over the skillet (inside and out). Place the skillet upside down on the oven rack and heat for one hour. Allow the skillet to cool completely before handling it. Once seasoned, the skillet should look shiny and smooth. Handwash and dry promptly to prevent rusting.

Mindful Eating

If you don't feel healthy, it's really hard to create happiness in other areas of your life. But our health isn't only about what we eat. Yes, proper nutrition is a key part of it, but *the way we eat* also affects our health. When we slow down and eat mindfully, we get the most nutrition and enjoyment from our food.

Slow down. I have been known to be a bit of a bulldozer at meals, quickly plowing through my food. However, the more I practice mindful eating, the more I realize that the digestive ailments I had been experiencing (bloating, stomachaches, etc.) were actually caused by eating too fast. Not only does eating slowly benefit your digestion and allow your body to properly absorb the nutrients in your food, but it also gives you time to savor the flavors and connect with your eating companions as well.

Take smaller bites. Many of us are used to gulping big mouthfuls and eating quickly due to busy schedules. Challenge yourself to take smaller bites and truly chew your food. Smaller bites will not only help you be present and slow down, but if you are really enjoying your food, it also means you get to enjoy the yummy item longer!

Do one thing at a time. You cannot eat mindfully while driving, typing, reading e-mail, or watching television. These activities are mutually exclusive. Our bodies and minds were not meant to do ten things at once. Although I admit to being completely guilty of multitasking, there is a huge benefit to just focusing on meals. Take the time to look at your food, smell it, pick it up, and put it back down. Taste it by moving it around your mouth and notice the different flavors that different areas of your tongue picks up. Take deep breaths, fully swallow between bites, and put your fork down. *What are you noticing in your body?*

Use internal, not external, cues to guide your eating. Are you *really* hungry, or are you just _____? (fill in the blank): stressed, tired, anxious, bored, eating because it's a certain time, eating because someone else is. So much of our eating experience is determined by the environment around us. Have you ever noticed that even if you don't like a particular food, if it is in front of you long enough, you will start snacking on it? A lot of our eating happens mindlessly; it's time to tune in to our bodies. Pay closer attention to your body and let it tell you when it's ready to eat.

Try different utensils. Do you eat more mindfully with chopsticks than with a fork? What about using your hands? I love using chopsticks, and they make it much easier for me to pay attention to how I am eating. This book contains a lot of noodle dishes that are easy to eat with chopsticks or a fork. Experiment and see how different utensils affect the way you experience your meal.

Ceramic is a nice alternative to cast iron, especially if you struggle with the weight of a cast iron skillet. Look for 100 percent ceramic cookware to ensure it does not have a nonstick coating. To keep your veggie noodles from sticking to the pan, be sure to follow the recipe instructions and add a bit of oil or sauce to the pan first.

Stainless steel is another fabulous alternative to cast iron; it cooks evenly, heats quickly, is dishwasher safe, and is long-lasting. As with cast iron or ceramic, be sure to add a bit of oil or sauce (as directed in the recipe) to make sure the noodles do not stick.

TONGS

If you're new to spiralizing, get yourself a pair of tongs. I've found them to be especially helpful when cooking zucchini noodles, because you can pull the noodles out, hold them over the pan, and allow them to drain before tossing them with the sauce or the rest of the dish.

VEGETABLE PEELER

Some vegetables should be peeled before spiralizing. To get the most from your spiralizer, make sure you have a standard handheld vegetable peeler.

WOODEN SPOONS

I prefer to use wooden spoons rather than metal when I'm cooking. One of the benefits of wood is that since it's not conductive, even if you leave your spoon in a hot soup the handle will stay cool. Another benefit is that wooden spoons won't scratch the surface of your pots and pans.

Tips for Spiralizer Success

Spiralizing is a great way to introduce new foods into your diet and replace less-healthy meals with healthier options. I have tried to vary the types of produce included in the recipes, with the idea of tempting you to try foods that you might never have tasted or cooked with before. While you can always substitute a more familiar item, I encourage you to try new vegetables. After all, you might be pleasantly surprised and even find a new favorite.

While we're on the subject of trying new things, I realize spiralizing might be completely new for you as well. So before we get to the recipes, here are some tips to make it easier.

SUCTION CUPS ARE YOUR BEST FRIEND

That heading sounds a little weird, but it's completely true! For a long time, I never used the suction cups on my hand-crank spiralizer, and spiralizing hard vegetables like carrots and sweet potatoes was such a pain. Make it easier on yourself by always using the suction cups, so the machine is stable and spiralizing hard veggies is a breeze.

Depending on your model, the suction cups may not easily stick to certain types of surfaces, for instance the wooden surface of a kitchen cart. If the spiralizer doesn't hold well, try switching to a different surface.

PLAN AND PREP AHEAD

The best advice I have for anyone trying to eat healthier and/or cook more at home is to have a plan. When I'm on top of my game, I sit down at the start of each week and draft out a loose meal plan (allowing some room for a meal out here and there), so I know exactly what I need to buy for the week. This is especially helpful for spiralizing, because you'll know what types of produce you need to pick up at the grocery store or farmers' market. I also like to have a day when I do most of my meal prep in advance, so I'll spiralize enough produce for several meals and store it all in the fridge. That way I can save time and easily prepare dinners throughout the week.

COOK ONCE, EAT TWICE

This is another great time-saving tip that has made a huge difference in my life. Whenever I cook, I typically double the recipe so I have another meal ready that only requires reheating. If I know that my schedule is particularly hectic, I'll even triple a recipe and freeze the extra so I can pull some out of the freezer and have a fresh, homemade meal ready to go. Freezing works best with items like soups, stews, and curries. If you plan to freeze a dish that calls for zucchini noodles, omit the noodles and make a fresh batch when you defrost the rest of the dish, to avoid mushy zoodles.

EAT 'EM RAW

It's funny to think about now, but for the first two years that I owned my spiralizer, I only ate my veggie noodles raw. While I love the flavor and texture of cooked vegetable noodles, I also love that they can be eaten raw to add a bit more crunch to meals. If you're looking to save on cooking time or add a bit more interest to a dish, feel free to enjoy your noodles raw!

MAKE IT YOURS

I've found that people usually fall into one of two camps: those who have a hard time following a recipe (me) and those who love to follow a recipe exactly. Regardless of which camp you're in, I encourage you to mix and match ingredients and flavor profiles to suit your tastes. The recipes are versatile, so substitute ingredients to use up produce you have on hand, add more or less salt, change the spices, or switch the type of blade if you're craving a particular type of noodle.

2

Classic Pastas

Smoky Mac and "Cheese"

SERVES 4 / PREP TIME: 10 MINUTES
COOK TIME: 20 MINUTES

EQUIPMENT NEEDED: FETTUCCINE BLADE

One of my all-time favorite restaurants in Seattle is Plum Bistro, a locally owned vegan restaurant in the Capitol Hill neighborhood. Their signature dish is a vegan mac and cheese that is so amazing, even the most hard-core cheese lover will swear it actually contains cheese. This recipe is inspired by that dish— minus the soy and gluten.

2 tablespoons coconut oil, divided
1 medium onion, finely diced
4 garlic cloves, minced
2 teaspoons smoked paprika
1 teaspoon ground cumin
1 teaspoon sea salt
2 cups vegetable broth
½ cup raw cashews
2 heaping tablespoons nutritional yeast flakes
2 medium yams, peeled, spiralized with the
    fettuccine blade
Freshly ground black pepper

1. Heat 1 tablespoon of the coconut oil in a large saucepan over medium heat. Add the onion and sauté for 5 minutes. Add the garlic, paprika, cumin, and salt and cook for 1 to 2 minutes, until the garlic is fragrant.

2. Put the onion and garlic mixture in a blender along with the vegetable broth, cashews, and nutritional yeast. Blend until smooth. Set aside.

3. Add the remaining 1 tablespoon of coconut oil to the pan over medium heat and add the yam noodles. Cook, stirring frequently, for 7 to 8 minutes, until the noodles are just tender. Add the sauce from the blender to the pan and cook, stirring frequently, for 2 to 3 minutes, until the noodles are tender and the sauce is hot.

4. Season with pepper and serve.

 Variation Tip: For a heartier meal, add roasted broccoli or a protein source of your choice.

Spaghetti with Mushroom Marinara

SERVES 4 / PREP TIME: 10 MINUTES
COOK TIME: 60 MINUTES

EQUIPMENT NEEDED: SPAGHETTI BLADE

Spaghetti with marinara sauce is a classic comfort food. This recipe takes an old favorite and transforms it into a healthy meal loaded with fresh vegetables. It's definitely a staple in my kitchen, and I have a feeling it might become a staple in yours as well.

2 tablespoons coconut oil, divided
1 medium onion, chopped
12 ounces cremini mushrooms, finely diced
4 garlic cloves, minced
2 medium carrots, peeled and finely diced
2 celery stalks, finely diced
1 teaspoon dried basil
1 teaspoon dried oregano
1 teaspoon dried thyme
1 teaspoon sea salt, plus more for final seasoning
1 (28-ounce) can diced tomatoes
¼ cup tomato paste
4 medium zucchini, spiralized with the spaghetti blade
Freshly ground black pepper

1. Heat 1 tablespoon of the coconut oil in a large pot over medium heat. Add the onion, mushrooms, garlic, carrots, celery, basil, oregano, thyme, and salt. Cook for 10 minutes, until the vegetables start to become tender and the spices are fragrant.

2. Add the diced tomatoes and their juice and the tomato paste. Bring to a boil, lower the heat to a simmer, and cook for 45 minutes, stirring occasionally.

3. While the sauce is cooking, heat the remaining 1 tablespoon of coconut oil in a medium skillet over medium heat. Add the zoodles and cook, stirring frequently, for 2 to 3 minutes, or until the zucchini reaches the texture you prefer. Drain the zucchini and set aside while the sauce finishes cooking.

4. Divide the zoodles among four plates and top with the sauce. Season with salt and pepper, and serve hot.

Cooking Tip: This is a great way to get more vegetables into your diet, especially if you cook for picky eaters. If there are mushroom-haters in the mix, you can also blend the sauce once it has cooked and simmered, so there are no visible mushroom chunks.

Cacio e Pepe with Lemon and Arugula

SERVES 2 TO 4 / PREP TIME: 10 MINUTES
COOK TIME: 5 MINUTES

EQUIPMENT NEEDED: SPAGHETTI BLADE

Cacio e pepe is a popular pasta dish from Rome. The name means "cheese and pepper." How do you make cacio e pepe with no cheese, you ask? You create the most incredible cashew "cheese," then add lemon juice to brighten the flavor, along with freshly ground black pepper for the traditional finish. (See tips for making sauces using raw cashews on page 23.)

1 tablespoon coconut oil

4 medium summer squash, spiralized with the spaghetti blade

½ cup raw whole cashews

1 tablespoon nutritional yeast

½ teaspoon sea salt

⅛ teaspoon garlic powder

⅛ teaspoon onion powder

3 tablespoons freshly squeezed lemon juice

2 tablespoons extra-virgin olive oil

4 cups baby arugula

Freshly ground black pepper

1. Heat the coconut oil in a medium skillet over medium heat. Add the summer squash noodles and cook for about 3 minutes, or until just tender, then drain the liquid from the pan. Set the squash noodles aside.

2. Combine the cashews, nutritional yeast, salt, garlic powder, and onion powder in a food processor and pulse until the cashews have the size and texture of grated parmesan cheese.

3. In a large bowl, combine the lemon juice, olive oil, arugula, and squash noodles, and mix well. Add the cashew "cheese" and toss.

4. Season with black pepper and serve.

Variation Tip: This recipe uses seasonal summer ingredients. If you want to enjoy it in the cooler months, try yam or butternut squash pasta along with a heartier green, like kale, in place of the summer squash noodles and baby arugula.

Green Bean Casserole with a Twist

VEGAN

SERVES 4 / PREP TIME: 10 MINUTES
COOK TIME: 20 MINUTES

EQUIPMENT NEEDED: SPAGHETTI AND
FETTUCCINE BLADES

This green bean casserole is a modern twist on the traditional favorite. It's cooked in a creamy cashew broth instead of canned soup and—possibly the best part—you don't have to actually bake it. It's meant to be cooked on the stove top, because if you're making this for the holidays, your oven is probably already overwhelmed.

1 tablespoon coconut oil
1 medium onion, spiralized with the fettuccine blade
2 cups vegetable broth
⅓ cup raw cashews
3 tablespoons nutritional yeast
1 teaspoon sea salt
3 garlic cloves, minced
½ pound green beans, trimmed and chopped
2 medium parsnips, peeled, spiralized with the spaghetti blade
1 medium sweet potato, peeled, spiralized with the spaghetti blade

1. Heat the coconut oil in a medium skillet over medium heat. Add the onion and cook for about 20 minutes, stirring occasionally, until it is caramelized and browned. Set aside.

2. While the onion is cooking, combine the vegetable broth, cashews, nutritional yeast, and salt in a blender. Blend until smooth.

3. Add the cashew broth to a large saucepan over medium-high heat. Add the garlic, green beans, parsnip noodles, and sweet potato noodles. Bring the sauce to a boil, reduce the heat, and simmer for about 15 minutes, stirring frequently, until all the vegetables are tender.

4. Transfer the vegetable mixture to a serving platter and top with the onion noodles. Serve warm.

Cooking Tip: You can also bake this dish. In step 3, pour everything into a baking pan, cover with foil, and bake at 350°F for 45 to 60 minutes, or until the noodles are tender. Remove from the oven and top with the onion noodles.

Tuna Casserole

SERVES 4 / PREP TIME: 10 MINUTES
COOK TIME: 1 HOUR, 15 MINUTES

EQUIPMENT NEEDED: SPAGHETTI BLADE

If the words "tuna casserole" don't sound appetizing, let me assure you, this is nothing like your grandmother's tuna casserole. It's full of roasted vegetables and a creamy cashew sauce. This recipe is also great with a bit of smoked paprika or hot sauce.

2 tablespoons coconut oil, divided

1 medium onion, finely diced

5 garlic cloves, minced

2 cups vegetable broth

⅓ cup raw cashews

1 teaspoon sea salt, plus more for final seasoning

2 medium parsnips, peeled, spiralized with the spaghetti blade

2 (5-ounce) cans tuna, drained

Freshly ground black pepper

3 scallions, white and green parts, chopped

1. Preheat the oven to 350°F.

2. Heat 1 tablespoon of the coconut oil in a medium skillet over medium heat. Add the onion and garlic, and sauté, stirring frequently, for 5 minutes or until fragrant.

3. In a blender, combine the onion and garlic mixture with the vegetable broth, cashews, and salt. Blend until smooth. Set aside.

4. Grease the bottom and sides of an 8-inch-square baking dish with the remaining 1 tablespoon of coconut oil. Put the parsnip noodles and tuna in the baking dish and mix well. Pour the cashew sauce on top.

5. Cover the baking dish with foil and bake for 1 hour. Remove the foil and bake for 5 to 10 minutes, or until the sauce has thickened slightly.

6. Season with salt and pepper, and serve hot, topped with the scallions.

Ingredient Tip: Look for tuna that is sustainably caught by pole or line fishing and does not have other liquids or fillers added.

Pappardelle with Turkey and Fennel Ragù

SERVES 4 / PREP TIME: 10 MINUTES
COOK TIME: 45 MINUTES

EQUIPMENT NEEDED: SPAGHETTI AND
RIBBON BLADES

I was first introduced to fresh fennel while working at a juice bar in college, and instantly fell in love with the sweet anise flavor it added to juices. Since then, I've added it to soups and salads, or slow roasted it with oil, salt, and pepper (heaven!). Fennel adds a unique flavor to the classic ragù. I like to make a double batch and freeze half for an easy meal later in the week.

1 small fennel bulb, green stems removed and
     reserved, bulb spiralized with the spaghetti blade
2 tablespoons coconut oil, divided
1 pound ground turkey
1 medium onion, finely diced
3 garlic cloves, minced
1 teaspoon dried basil
1 teaspoon dried oregano
1 teaspoon dried thyme
½ teaspoon fennel seeds
¼ teaspoon red pepper flakes
1 teaspoon sea salt, plus more for final seasoning
1 (28-ounce) can diced tomatoes
2 tablespoons tomato paste
4 medium summer squash, spiralized with the
     ribbon blade
Freshly ground black pepper

1. Dice the fennel stems and set them aside.

2. Heat 1 tablespoon of the coconut oil in a large pot over medium heat and add the turkey. Cook, stirring frequently, for 10 minutes, or until the turkey is well browned.

3. Drain any excess fat from the pan and add the onion, garlic, spiralized fennel, diced fennel stems, basil, oregano, thyme, fennel seeds, red pepper flakes, and salt. Cook, stirring frequently, for 5 minutes, until the onion is tender and the spices are fragrant.

4. Add the diced tomatoes and their juice and the tomato paste. Bring to a boil, lower the heat to a simmer, and cook for 30 minutes, stirring occasionally.

5. While the sauce is cooking, heat the remaining 1 tablespoon of coconut oil in a medium skillet over medium heat. Add the summer squash ribbons and cook, stirring frequently, for 2 to 3 minutes, or until the squash reaches the texture you prefer.

6. Divide the squash among four plates and top with the ragù. Season with salt and pepper, and serve hot.

Ingredient Tip: Fennel is in season in late fall and early spring. Choose one that is bright white, without any loose outer layers or bruises, and has a firm bulb and stems, not limp or rubbery.

Fettuccine Alfredo

SERVES 4 / PREP TIME: 10 MINUTES
COOK TIME: 20 MINUTES

EQUIPMENT NEEDED: FETTUCCINE BLADE

This recipe was created on a particularly dreary fall Saturday when I emerged from the farmers' market carrying two giant bunches of kale and a pound of fresh rutabagas. What to do with all that produce? The kale was transformed into kale chips, which were devoured while watching Orange Is the New Black. *The rutabagas became pasta, which deserved its own dairy-free Alfredo sauce. This dish is also fabulous in summer. The sauce is great over zucchini pasta.*

2 tablespoons coconut oil, divided

1 pound boneless, skinless chicken thighs or breasts, cut into strips

4 medium rutabagas, peeled, spiralized with the fettuccine blade

3 cups cauliflower florets

¼ cup raw whole cashews

½ teaspoon garlic powder

½ teaspoon onion powder

1 cup plus 2 tablespoons vegetable broth

1 teaspoon sea salt, plus more for final seasoning

1 tablespoon freshly squeezed lemon juice

Freshly ground black pepper

1. Heat 1 tablespoon of the coconut oil in a medium skillet over medium heat. Add the chicken and cook for 8 to 10 minutes, stirring occasionally. When the chicken has reached an internal temperature of at least 165°F, remove from the heat.

2. Heat the remaining 1 tablespoon of coconut oil in a large saucepan over medium heat. Add the rutabaga noodles and cook, stirring occasionally, for 8 to 10 minutes, or until just tender.

3. While the rutabaga pasta is cooking, fill a medium pot about halfway with water and bring to a boil over high heat. Put the cauliflower in a steamer basket and steam for 5 to 7 minutes, until the cauliflower is tender.

4. Combine the cooked cauliflower, cashews, garlic powder, onion powder, broth, salt, and lemon juice in a blender and blend until smooth.

5. Add the sauce and cooked chicken to the saucepan with the rutabaga pasta and simmer for about 5 minutes, until the sauce is hot and the noodles are tender. Season with salt and pepper, and serve hot.

Variation Tip: If you're new to dairy-free sauces and are craving a "cheesier" flavor, try increasing the cashews to ⅓ cup and adding 2 tablespoons of nutritional yeast.

Sausage and Sun-Dried Tomato Pasta

SERVES 4 / PREP TIME: 15 MINUTES
COOK TIME: 25 MINUTES

EQUIPMENT NEEDED: SPAGHETTI BLADE

There's nothing more satisfying than a creamy sun-dried tomato sauce served over a bed of pasta, especially when the sauce contains no actual cream and the pasta is really just vegetables. Chiffonade *is the French term for "cut into long, thin strips." Simply stack the basil leaves on top of one another, roll them up tightly, and cut the roll into thin slices.*

3 heaping cups cauliflower florets

2 tablespoons coconut oil, divided

3 garlic cloves, minced

1 medium onion, finely diced

¼ cup sun-dried tomatoes

1 teaspoon ground cumin

2 tablespoons tomato paste

1 cup full-fat unsweetened canned coconut milk

¼ cup vegetable broth

1 teaspoon sea salt

¼ teaspoon freshly ground black pepper

1 pound ground Italian sausage

4 medium zucchini, spiralized with the spaghetti blade

¼ cup fresh basil, cut into chiffonade

1. Fill a medium pot about halfway with water and bring to a boil over high heat. Put the cauliflower in a steamer basket and steam for 5 to 7 minutes, until it is tender.

2. While the cauliflower is steaming, heat 1 tablespoon of the coconut oil in a medium skillet over medium heat. Add the garlic, onion, sun-dried tomatoes, and cumin, and sauté for about 5 minutes. Put the mixture in a blender.

3. When the cauliflower is tender, add it to the blender as well. Add the tomato paste, coconut milk, vegetable broth, salt, and pepper. Process everything until smooth.

4. Add the remaining 1 tablespoon of coconut oil to the same skillet, and place it over medium heat. Crumble the sausage into the pan and cook for 7 to 8 minutes, or until the meat is golden brown and the internal temperature reaches at least 145°F. Add the sun-dried tomato sauce from the blender and let it simmer for 2 to 3 minutes, until the sauce is hot.

5. In a separate pan over medium heat, add a bit of the sauce and the zucchini noodles. Sauté for 3 minutes, until just tender, and drain any liquid from the pan.

6. Divide the zoodles among four bowls and top with the sun-dried tomato sauce, and basil.

Spaghetti with Meatballs

SERVES 4 / PREP TIME: 15 MINUTES
COOK TIME: 50 MINUTES

EQUIPMENT NEEDED: SPAGHETTI BLADE

I usually make a double or triple batch of these meatballs so I can freeze the extras for easy future meals. This recipe is for a busy week-night, when making a sauce from scratch sounds like a bit too much, so it calls for a jar of premade marinara sauce instead. Be sure to look for a brand that is organic and does not contain any added sugar.

4 tablespoons coconut oil, divided
½ medium onion, finely diced
2 garlic cloves, minced
1 teaspoon sea salt
½ teaspoon dried basil
½ teaspoon freshly ground black pepper
½ teaspoon dried rosemary, crushed
½ teaspoon dried thyme
¼ teaspoon red pepper flakes
¼ cup fresh parsley, finely chopped
½ cup almond flour, divided
1 pound grass-fed ground beef
1 free-range egg, beaten
1 (24-ounce) jar marinara sauce
4 medium zucchini, spiralized with the spaghetti blade

1. Heat 1 tablespoon of the coconut oil in a skillet over medium heat. Add the onion and sauté for 5 minutes, until translucent. Add the garlic and sauté for 1 minute. Remove from the heat and set aside.

2. Put the salt, basil, black pepper, rosemary, thyme, red pepper flakes, parsley, and ¼ cup of almond flour in a large bowl and mix. Add the onion and garlic, ground beef, and egg to the bowl and thoroughly mix all the ingredients. Form the mixture into 12 medium meatballs.

3. Spread the remaining ¼ cup of the almond flour out on a plate. Roll the meatballs in the flour until thoroughly coated.

4. Heat 2 tablespoons of the coconut oil in the skillet over medium heat. Add half the meatballs and brown for 15 minutes, flipping every 5 minutes to ensure that every side is evenly cooked. Cook the meatballs in two batches to prevent overcrowding.

5. When all the meatballs are cooked, place them in a large saucepan and pour in the marinara sauce. Simmer over low heat for 10 minutes, until the sauce is heated through.

6. While the sauce is simmering, heat the remaining 1 tablespoon of coconut oil in another saucepan over medium heat and add the zoodles. Sauté for 3 minutes, until just tender, and drain any liquid from the pan.

7. Divide the zoodles between four bowls and top with hot marinara and meatballs. Serve immediately.

Cooking Tip: This is a great recipe to introduce zucchini pasta to the family. I typically recommend keeping the skin on the zucchini, but if the green color makes family members hesitant, you can always peel the zucchini before spiralizing so it resembles the color of wheat pasta.

Spaghetti with Beef Bolognese

SERVES 4 / PREP TIME: 5 MINUTES
COOK TIME: 45 MINUTES

EQUIPMENT NEEDED: SPAGHETTI BLADE

Need a quick weeknight dinner? This is it. This meat sauce is a great one to double or triple, storing the extra in the freezer for the following week. In the morning, I'll transfer the frozen sauce to the refrigerator to thaw while I'm at work; then all I have to do is make a fresh batch of zucchini pasta and dinner is ready.

2 tablespoons coconut oil, divided
1 pound grass-fed ground beef
1 medium onion, chopped
4 garlic cloves, minced
1 teaspoon dried basil
1 teaspoon dried oregano
1 teaspoon dried thyme
1 teaspoon sea salt, plus more for final seasoning
1 (28-ounce) can diced tomatoes
¼ cup tomato paste
4 medium zucchini, spiralized with the spaghetti blade
Freshly ground black pepper

1. Heat 1 tablespoon of the coconut oil in a large pot over medium heat and add the ground beef. Cook, stirring frequently, for 10 minutes, until the beef is well browned.

2. Drain any excess fat from the pan and add the onion, garlic, basil, oregano, thyme, and salt. Cook, stirring frequently, for 5 minutes, until the onion is tender and the spices are fragrant.

3. Add the diced tomatoes and their juice and the tomato paste. Bring to a boil, then lower the heat to a simmer and cook for 30 minutes, stirring occasionally.

4. While the sauce is cooking, heat the remaining 1 tablespoon of coconut oil in a medium skillet over medium heat. Add the zucchini noodles and cook, stirring frequently, for 2 to 3 minutes, or until the zoodles reach the texture you prefer. Drain them and set aside until the sauce is ready.

5. Divide the zoodles among four plates and top with the sauce. Season with salt and pepper, and serve hot.

Cooking Tip: Put your zucchini scraps to use! Grab any squash left over after spiralizing, chop, and add to the sauce with the canned tomatoes so they don't go to waste.

Beef Stroganoff

SERVES 4 / PREP TIME: 15 MINUTES
COOK TIME: 35 MINUTES

EQUIPMENT NEEDED: SPAGHETTI BLADE

This incredible combination of savory, salty, and creamy flavors delights me every time! Instead of the traditional beef stroganoff recipe with cream, butter, and lots of white flour, this one uses fresh cremini mushrooms, broth, onions, garlic, and sea salt. This satisfying dish can be ready in under an hour, and you can even make a double batch of the sauce and freeze half to reheat later.

2 tablespoons coconut oil, divided
1 pound grass-fed beef sirloin tips
1 medium onion, finely diced
3 garlic cloves, minced
8 ounces cremini mushrooms, sliced
1⅓ cups beef broth
½ teaspoon sea salt, plus more for final seasoning
4 medium zucchini, spiralized with the spaghetti blade
⅓ cup raw cashews
1 teaspoon arrowroot powder
Freshly ground black pepper

1. Heat 1 tablespoon of the coconut oil in a large pot over medium heat. Add the beef and sauté for 5 minutes, until it just starts to brown. Add the onion, garlic, and mushrooms, and sauté for an additional 5 minutes, until the onion and garlic are fragrant.

2. Add 1 cup of the beef broth and the salt, bring to a boil, then reduce the heat and simmer, covered, for 20 minutes, or until the beef is tender.

3. While the beef is cooking, heat the remaining 1 tablespoon of oil in a skillet over medium heat. Add the zucchini noodles and sauté until just tender, 3 to 5 minutes. Drain the zoodles and set aside until the sauce is ready.

4. Add the remaining ⅓ cup of beef broth to a blender, along with the cashews, and blend until smooth. When the beef is tender, stir in the blended cashew broth and whisk in the arrowroot powder. Simmer for 1 to 2 minutes, until the sauce thickens, then remove from the heat.

5. Serve the beef and sauce over the zoodles. Season with salt and pepper, and serve hot.

Make It Vegan: Use vegetable broth, leave out the beef, and add extra mushrooms or your favorite vegetarian protein source.

3

Creative Pastas

45

Fettuccine with Rosemary Butternut Crème Sauce

SERVES 4 / PREP TIME: 10 MINUTES
COOK TIME: 25 MINUTES

EQUIPMENT NEEDED: FETTUCCINE BLADE

This is one of my favorite recipes that I have adapted many times over the years. I featured a version of this dish on my blog in 2013 that to date has been shared more than 400,000 times. I don't think I'm alone when I say this recipe is one of the best things that's ever happened to fall.

2 cups peeled and chopped butternut squash

1 medium onion, chopped

2 garlic cloves, minced

1 cup full-fat unsweetened canned coconut milk

1 cup vegetable or chicken broth

1 teaspoon dried rosemary, crushed

½ teaspoon sea salt

1 teaspoon arrowroot powder

1 tablespoon coconut oil

4 medium zucchini, spiralized with the spaghetti blade

1. Combine the butternut squash, onion, garlic, coconut milk, broth, rosemary, and salt in a medium pot. Bring everything to a boil, lower the heat, and simmer, covered, for 15 to 20 minutes, or until the butternut squash is tender. Put the squash mixture in a blender and blend until smooth.

2. Return the sauce to the pot and over medium heat, whisk in the arrowroot powder. Simmer for 1 to 2 minutes, until the sauce is thick. Set aside.

3. Heat the coconut oil in a medium skillet over medium heat. Add the zoodles and cook, stirring frequently, for 3 to 5 minutes, or until they are tender. Drain the zoodles and divide among four plates. Top with the sauce.

Substitution Tip: If zucchini is not in season, try substituting a seasonal root vegetable like parsnip, sweet potatoes, or celeriac. Peel before spiralizing.

Pasta with Carrot-Cashew Crème Sauce

SERVES 4 / PREP TIME: 10 MINUTES
COOK TIME: 15 MINUTES

EQUIPMENT NEEDED: SPAGHETTI BLADE

Asparagus and zucchini in a carrot-cashew crème sauce? This unconventional cream sauce is made from fresh carrot juice and cashews, creating an incredibly sweet and creamy combination.

2 tablespoons coconut oil, divided
½ medium onion, finely diced
3 garlic cloves, minced
½ cup fresh carrot juice
1 cup raw cashews
½ cup water
¾ teaspoon sea salt, plus more for final seasoning
1 bunch asparagus (tough ends snapped off), sliced
4 medium zucchini, spiralized with the spaghetti blade
Freshly ground black pepper

1. Heat 1 tablespoon of the coconut oil in a medium skillet over medium heat. Add the onion and sauté for 5 minutes. Add the garlic and sauté for 1 minute. Combine the onion, garlic, carrot juice, cashews, water, and salt in a blender and process until smooth.

2. Pour the sauce into a large saucepan and over medium-low heat, simmer for 5 minutes, until the sauce is hot.

3. Heat the remaining 1 tablespoon of coconut oil in the same skillet over medium heat. Add the asparagus and sauté for 5 minutes. Add the zoodles to the saucepan and sauté for 3 minutes, until they are just tender. Drain any liquid from the pan.

4. Divide the zoodles and asparagus among four plates and top with the sauce. Season with salt and pepper.

Substitution Tip: Is asparagus out of season? Try mushrooms, snap peas, or sliced red radishes instead.

Leek and Sage Crème Sauce over Pasta

SERVES 4 / PREP TIME: 10 MINUTES
COOK TIME: 20 MINUTES

EQUIPMENT NEEDED: SPAGHETTI BLADE

In 2012 I made a wonderful culinary discovery when I realized that you can blend cauliflower into sauces to create some of the qualities of a traditional cream sauce. This version combines cauliflower with a touch of coconut milk and sage for a truly satisfying dish that goes great on top of any veggie pasta. Leeks are part of the Allium *family and look like a giant scallion.*

1 tablespoon coconut oil

1 medium leek, white parts only, cleaned
    and chopped

3 garlic cloves, minced

3 heaping cups cauliflower florets

2 tablespoons apple cider vinegar

1 cup full-fat unsweetened canned coconut milk

1 teaspoon sea salt, plus more for final seasoning

1 teaspoon ground cumin

2 tablespoons chopped fresh sage leaves

1 large butternut squash, bulbous end removed,
    top part peeled then spiralized with the
    spaghetti blade

Freshly ground black pepper

1. Heat the coconut oil in a large saucepan over medium-low heat. Add the leek and sauté for 5 minutes, watching carefully to ensure it does not burn. Add the garlic and sauté for 1 minute.

2. Steam the cauliflower florets for 5 minutes, or until tender. When the cauliflower is tender, transfer it to a blender. Add the cooked leeks, apple cider vinegar, coconut milk, salt, and cumin and process until smooth.

3. Return the sauce to the saucepan. Add the sage and butternut squash noodles. Cook over medium heat, stirring frequently, for 10 to 15 minutes, or until the butternut squash pasta is tender.

4. Season with salt and pepper and serve hot.

Ingredient Tip: Spiralizing a large butternut squash can be a bit tricky. To make this easier, cut off the bulbous end of the squash and set it aside. Then peel the top part, lay the squash on its side, and cut it in half before placing on the spiralizer. To ensure no squash is wasted (since the bulbous end cannot be spiralized), I like to scoop the seeds out of the bulbous end, peel and dice it, and refrigerate it for another dish.

Truffle Pasta with Kale and Roasted Cauliflower

VEGAN

SERVES 4 / PREP TIME: 15 MINUTES
COOK TIME: 20 MINUTES

EQUIPMENT NEEDED: SPAGHETTI BLADE

This pasta is pure comfort food, with a twist. Anytime I serve this to friends, they're always amazed that it doesn't contain any dairy! Instead, the creamy sauce is made by blending onions and garlic with cashews, veggie broth, and sea salt. The final dish is tossed with a bit of truffle oil for a rich and decadent flavor that will satisfy your taste buds without making your body feel heavy.

1 large head cauliflower, cut into bite-size florets

2 tablespoons coconut oil, divided

1 medium onion, finely diced

3 garlic cloves, minced

⅓ cup raw cashews

2 cups vegetable broth

1 teaspoon sea salt

2 medium sweet potatoes, peeled, spiralized with the spaghetti blade

4 large curly kale leaves, stemmed and chopped

1 teaspoon truffle oil

Freshly ground black pepper

2 teaspoons chopped fresh thyme leaves

1. Preheat the oven to 375°F.

2. Toss the cauliflower with 1 tablespoon of the coconut oil and spread it out in a single layer on a baking sheet. Roast for about 20 minutes, flipping at least once, until the cauliflower is golden and tender.

3. While the cauliflower is roasting, heat the remaining 1 tablespoon of coconut oil in a large saucepan over medium heat. Add the onion and garlic and sauté, stirring frequently, for 5 minutes, or until fragrant.

4. Put the onion and garlic mixture, cashews, broth, and salt in a blender. Blend until smooth.

5. Return the sauce to the saucepan, along with the sweet potato noodles and kale. Cover the pan and simmer over medium heat for 6 to 8 minutes, stirring frequently, until the sweet potato is cooked and the kale is tender. Mix in the roasted cauliflower and stir in the truffle oil.

6. Season with black pepper, garnish with the fresh thyme, and serve hot.

Variation Tip: If you want a lighter dish, substitute 4 medium zucchini for the sweet potatoes. Cook the zucchini in coconut oil or 1 cup vegetable broth for 3 to 5 minutes until tender, drain, and toss with the sauce.

Pasta with Five-Minute Tomato Sauce

VEGAN

SERVES 4 / PREP TIME: 10 MINUTES

EQUIPMENT NEEDED: SPAGHETTI BLADE

Did you know that you can enjoy zucchini pasta without even cooking it? It's true! This recipe comes from my past life when I was a raw vegan for a hot minute, and uses a few fresh ingredients to create a creamy tomato sauce right in your blender. For a heartier entrée, pair this with your favorite protein source. This sauce goes equally well with grilled fish or a grilled portobello mushroom.

5 medium Roma tomatoes
2 medium garlic cloves, minced
¼ cup tahini
1 tablespoon dried basil
1 tablespoon dried oregano
1 teaspoon sea salt, plus more for final seasoning
2 tablespoons sun-dried tomatoes
4 medium zucchini, spiralized with the spaghetti blade
1½ cups cherry tomatoes, halved
Freshly ground black pepper

1. Combine the tomatoes, garlic, tahini, basil, oregano, salt, and sun-dried tomatoes in a blender. Blend until smooth.

2. Divide the zoodles among four bowls. Top with the tomato sauce and the cherry tomatoes.

3. Season with salt and pepper, and serve immediately.

Ingredient Tip: Tahini is a paste made from crushed sesame seeds. You can find it in supermarkets and health food stores.

Pasta with Mushroom Sauce

VEGAN

SERVES 4 / PREP TIME: 10 MINUTES
COOK TIME: 15 MINUTES

EQUIPMENT NEEDED: SPAGHETTI BLADE

Have you ever tried turnips? If they're new to you, don't worry, most folks probably hadn't either until Michelle Obama put them on the map with her famous #TurnipForWhat video (https://vine.co/tags/TurnipForWhat). Turnips are a root vegetable with a large white and purple bulb. You'll find them at farmers' markets in fall and in many grocery stores year-round.

2 tablespoons coconut oil, divided
2 large turnips, peeled, spiralized with the
    spaghetti blade
12 ounces cremini mushrooms, sliced
2 medium shallots, chopped
3 garlic cloves, minced
2 tablespoons tomato paste
2 cups vegetable broth
⅓ cup raw cashews
½ teaspoon sea salt, plus more for final seasoning
1 teaspoon red wine vinegar
1 teaspoon arrowroot powder
1 tablespoon chopped fresh thyme leaves
Freshly ground black pepper

1. Heat 1 tablespoon of the coconut oil in a large skillet over medium heat. Add the turnip pasta and cook, stirring frequently, for about 10 minutes, or until tender.

2. While the turnip pasta is cooking, put the remaining 1 tablespoon of coconut oil in a large saucepan over medium heat. Add the mushrooms, shallots, and garlic and cook, stirring frequently, for 5 to 7 minutes, until the mushrooms are browned and the garlic and shallots are fragrant.

3. Put the tomato paste, broth, cashews, salt, and red wine vinegar in a blender. Blend until smooth.

4. Add the cashew sauce to the mushrooms and set over medium heat. Whisk in the arrowroot and thyme, and simmer for 1 to 2 minutes, until the sauce is thick. Add the cooked turnip noodles to the sauce and cook another minute.

5. Season with salt and pepper, and serve hot.

Ingredient Tip: Turnips tend to get a bad rap due to their slightly spicy flavor, but their spiciness mellows when cooked, and is masked well by this creamy sauce. However, if you're not a fan, substitute another seasonal vegetable of your choice.

Pasta with Lemon-Crème Sauce and Salmon

SERVES 4 / PREP TIME: 15 MINUTES
COOK TIME: 25 MINUTES

EQUIPMENT NEEDED: SPAGHETTI BLADE

This is a great dinner for a special occasion; there's something fancy about salmon with beet pasta and a cream sauce. If you're looking to impress a date, this is definitely one of the recipes that comes to mind!

4 large beets, peeled, spiralized with the
  spaghetti blade
3 tablespoons coconut oil, divided
1 medium onion, chopped
3 garlic cloves, minced
3 heaping cups cauliflower florets
¼ cup freshly squeezed lemon juice
1 tablespoon freshly grated lemon zest
1 cup full-fat unsweetened canned coconut milk
1 teaspoon sea salt, plus pinch
3 teaspoons ground cumin, divided
1 teaspoon garlic powder
1 teaspoon mustard powder
1 teaspoon smoked paprika
Freshly ground black pepper
4 (4 to 6 ounce) salmon fillets

1. Preheat the oven to 350°F.

2. Toss the beet noodles with 1 tablespoon of the coconut oil. Spread them out in an even layer on a baking sheet and roast for about 15 minutes, or until the noodles are tender but not dry.

3. While the beet noodles are roasting, heat 1 tablespoon of the coconut oil in a medium skillet
over medium heat. Add the onion and cook for 5 minutes. Add the garlic and sauté for 1 minute.

4. Steam the cauliflower florets for 5 minutes, or until tender. When the cauliflower is tender, transfer it to a blender. Put the cooked onion and garlic, the lemon juice, lemon zest, coconut milk, 1 teaspoon salt, and 1 teaspoon of cumin in a blender and process until smooth. Set aside.

5. Mix the remaining 2 teaspoons of cumin, the garlic powder, mustard powder, paprika, and a pinch of salt and pepper together in a small bowl. Sprinkle it over the salmon and rub it in.

6. Heat the remaining 1 tablespoon of coconut oil over medium heat in the same skillet. Add the salmon. Cook for about 5 minutes, then carefully turn the fish over. Continue cooking for 5 minutes, or until the internal temperature reaches 135°F.

7. Divide the beets among four plates and top with the sauce and salmon. Serve hot.

Substitution Tip: If you're not a fan of the very red mess left from spiralizing red beets, try golden beets instead, or substitute another root vegetable of your choice.

Pasta with Caramelized Onions and Radicchio

SERVES 4 / PREP TIME: 10 MINUTES
COOK TIME: 20 MINUTES

EQUIPMENT NEEDED: SPAGHETTI AND
RIBBON BLADES

This dish simply tastes like fall. I love radicchio for its beautiful purple color and the slight bitterness it adds to dishes. This recipe uses naturally sweet vegetables, like sweet onions and sweet potatoes, along with healthy fat from olive oil, to balance the bitterness of the radicchio.

2 tablespoons coconut oil, divided
2 large onions, spiralized with the ribbon blade
1 teaspoon sea salt
1 small head radicchio, chopped
1 tablespoon balsamic vinegar
2 large sweet potatoes, peeled, spiralized with the spaghetti blade
2 tablespoons extra-virgin olive oil
¼ cup chopped flat-leaf parsley

1. Heat 1 tablespoon of the coconut oil in a large skillet over medium-low heat. Add the onions and salt. Cook, stirring occasionally, for 10 minutes.

2. Put the remaining 1 tablespoon of coconut oil in a separate skillet over medium-high heat. Add the radicchio and sear for about 3 minutes, or until the radicchio is browned on the edges. Lower the heat, stir in the balsamic vinegar, and sauté for 1 to 2 minutes, until the radicchio is slightly softened. Set aside.

3. Add the sweet potato noodles to the onions and cook for 8 to 10 minutes, stirring frequently, until the noodles are tender. Add the radicchio and mix well.

4. Drizzle with the olive oil and garnish with the parsley. Serve warm.

Substitution Tip: If you don't like bitter flavors or if you can't find radicchio, substitute a small head of red cabbage instead. Since red cabbage is denser than radicchio, you may have to increase the cooking time to 10 to 15 minutes, or until the cabbage has reached the texture you prefer.

Spicy Goulash

SERVES 4 / PREP TIME: 10 MINUTES
COOK TIME: 35 MINUTES

EQUIPMENT NEEDED: FETTUCCINE BLADE

This goulash is a hearty dish made with beef, spices, and spiralized sweet potato and zucchini. It's so filling that you won't even realize there are no wheat noodles in this dish!

1 tablespoon coconut oil

1 pound grass-fed ground beef

1 medium onion, chopped

3 garlic cloves, finely chopped

2 teaspoons smoked paprika

1½ teaspoons dried oregano

1 teaspoon dried basil

1 teaspoon sea salt

¾ teaspoon chili powder, or as desired

½ teaspoon dried thyme

1 (28-ounce) can diced tomatoes

4 tablespoons tomato paste

1 cup water or vegetable broth

1 medium sweet potato, peeled, spiralized
   with the fettuccine blade

1 medium zucchini, spiralized with the
   fettuccine blade

1. Heat the coconut oil in a large pot over medium heat and add the ground beef. Cook, stirring frequently, for 10 minutes, or until the beef is well browned. Drain any excess fat from the pot.

2. Add the onion, garlic, paprika, oregano, basil, salt, chili powder, and thyme. Cook, stirring frequently, for 5 minutes, until the onion is tender and the spices are fragrant.

3. Add the diced tomatoes and their juice, tomato paste, water, and sweet potato noodles. Bring to a boil, lower the heat to a simmer, and cook for 15 minutes, stirring occasionally. Add the zoodles and cook for 5 minutes, or until the vegetables are tender.

4. Serve hot.

Substitution Tip: If you're looking for a leaner dish, use ground turkey instead of the beef and/or another zucchini in place of the sweet potato.

4

Around the World in Noodles

Spicy Almond Noodles

SERVES 4 / PREP TIME: 10 MINUTES
COOK TIME: 5 MINUTES

EQUIPMENT NEEDED: SPAGHETTI BLADE

Do you ever have those days where you just want peanut sauce? I totally do. But if you have peanut allergies or are eating Paleo, peanuts are off the menu. This dish uses almond butter instead to create a creamy, delightful sauce. It might just be better than takeout.

1 tablespoon coconut oil

4 medium zucchini, spiralized with the spaghetti blade

1 large carrot, peeled, spiralized with the spaghetti blade

¼ cup almond butter

2 tablespoons coconut aminos

2 tablespoons honey or maple syrup

2 tablespoons freshly squeezed lime juice

2 tablespoons sesame oil

2 garlic cloves, minced

½-inch piece fresh ginger, grated

1 to 2 tablespoons hot sauce, or as desired

3 scallions, white and green parts, chopped

½ cup roasted cashews, chopped

1. Heat the coconut oil in a medium skillet over medium heat. Add the zucchini and carrot noodles and cook for 3 to 5 minutes, until tender but not mushy.

2. In a small bowl, mix the almond butter, coconut aminos, honey, lime juice, sesame oil, garlic, ginger, and hot sauce.

3. When the noodles are cooked, place them in a colander to drain any excess moisture. In a large bowl, toss the noodles with the almond butter sauce and scallions.

4. Top with the roasted cashews and serve warm.

Variation Tip: To make this a complete meal, try pairing it with grilled chicken, baked salmon, or a vegetarian protein source.

Cold Sesame Noodle Salad

VEGAN

SERVES 4 / PREP TIME: 10 MINUTES

EQUIPMENT NEEDED: SPAGHETTI AND
RIBBON BLADES

*This recipe has all of the traditional flavors
without any of the added sugar or wheat! Pair
it with a protein source of your choice for a
complete meal.*

2 medium cucumbers, spiralized with the
    spaghetti blade

2 tablespoons coconut aminos

2 tablespoons sesame oil

1 tablespoon almond butter

2 teaspoons freshly squeezed lime juice

1 garlic clove, minced

½-inch piece fresh ginger, grated

¼ teaspoon sea salt, plus more for final seasoning

1 medium red bell pepper, stemmed, spiralized with
    the ribbon blade, then seeded

1 large carrot, peeled, spiralized with the
    spaghetti blade

½ medium daikon radish, peeled, spiralized with the
    spaghetti blade

¼ cup chopped cilantro

2 scallions, white and green parts, chopped

2 tablespoons sesame seeds

Freshly ground black pepper

1. Place the cucumber noodles on paper towels to soak up any excess moisture. Set aside.

2. Mix the coconut aminos, sesame oil, almond butter, lime juice, garlic, ginger, and salt in a small bowl.

3. In a large bowl, mix the cucumber, bell pepper, carrot, and daikon noodles with the cilantro. Add the sesame oil dressing and mix well.

4. Garnish with the scallions and sesame seeds, and season with salt and pepper.

Substitution Tip: If daikon radish is out of season or hard to find, just add an extra carrot.

Kimchi Noodles

SERVES 4 / PREP TIME: 10 MINUTES
COOK TIME: 15 MINUTES

EQUIPMENT NEEDED: SPAGHETTI BLADE

*I love kimchi—spicy fermented cabbage—
for its unique taste as well as the probiotic
benefits. Since kimchi contains live bacteria,
to get the most benefit the kimchi should be
added at the end and not directly heated. Also,
some brands of kimchi contain fish sauce and/
or meat broth, so if you are vegetarian, be sure
to check the label.*

1 tablespoon coconut oil
3 baby bok choy, chopped
1 medium onion, diced
3 medium parsnips, peeled, spiralized with the
    spaghetti blade
2 garlic cloves, minced
1 tablespoon coconut aminos
3 scallions, white and green parts, chopped
1 cup kimchi, or as desired
Sea salt
Freshly ground black pepper

1. Heat the coconut oil in a large skillet over medium heat. Add the bok choy and onion and cook for about 5 minutes, until the onion is tender.

2. Add the parsnip noodles, garlic, and coconut aminos. Cook, stirring frequently, for 7 to 8 minutes, or until the noodles are tender. Turn off the heat, add the scallions and kimchi, and mix well.

3. Season with salt and pepper, and serve hot.

 Variation Tip: Make this dish a bit heartier by topping it with a fried egg. Yum!

Raw Veggie Sushi Bowl

VEGAN

SERVES 2 / PREP TIME: 10 MINUTES

EQUIPMENT NEEDED: SPAGHETTI AND
RIBBON BLADES

*These simple veggie sushi bowls have all the
familiar flavors of sushi without the work
associated with making the rolls—or the raw
fish! To make this a complete entrée, top a bowl
with grilled chicken or salmon.*

2 cucumbers, spiralized with the spaghetti blade

1 medium bell pepper, stemmed, spiralized with the
   ribbon blade, then seeded

1 medium carrot, peeled, spiralized with the
   spaghetti blade

1 medium avocado, pitted and sliced

2 (8-inch-square) sheets dried nori, cut into
   matchsticks

2 medium scallions, white and green parts, chopped

Sea salt

Freshly ground black pepper

Coconut aminos

Pickled ginger (optional)

Wasabi (optional)

1. Divide the cucumber, bell pepper, and carrot noodles between two bowls.

2. Top with the avocado, nori, and scallions. Season with salt and pepper.

3. Serve with coconut aminos for dipping. Offer the pickled ginger and wasabi on the side (if using).

Ingredient Tip: Nori are thin sheets of dried seaweed that are wrapped around rice and raw fish in sushi. You can find it at any Asian market, as well as many health food stores and grocery stores. It's a wonderful source of minerals and adds a savory flavor. Nori can be used as a wrap instead of tortillas or bread, or added to salads and other dishes.

Sweet Potato Yakisoba

VEGAN

SERVES 4 / PREP TIME: 10 MINUTES
COOK TIME: 10 MINUTES

EQUIPMENT NEEDED: SPAGHETTI AND
RIBBON BLADES

*Yakisoba is a popular Japanese fried noodle
dish of pan-fried ramen with pork, vegetables,
and sauce. This version combines elements of a
classic yakisoba, but uses sweet potatoes instead
of noodles and cabbage instead of meat.*

2 tablespoons coconut oil
½ medium onion, thinly sliced
2 garlic cloves, minced
1-inch piece fresh ginger, grated
2 medium sweet potatoes, peeled, spiralized with
    the spaghetti blade
1 carrot, peeled, spiralized the spaghetti blade
¼ cup coconut aminos
½ head green cabbage, spiralized with the
    ribbon blade
2 scallions, white and green parts, sliced
Sea salt
Freshly ground black pepper

1. Heat the coconut oil in a large pan over
medium heat. Add the onion, garlic, and
ginger, and sauté for 1 minute.

2. Add the sweet potato and carrot noodles,
and the coconut aminos. Cook for 5 to
7 minutes, stirring frequently, until the sweet
potatoes are tender and just starting to brown.

3. Add the cabbage ribbons and scallions, cook
for 1 to 2 minutes, and remove from the heat.

4. Season with salt and pepper. Serve hot.

Substitution Tip: For a low-carb version,
substitute 3 zucchini for the sweet potatoes.

Teriyaki Chicken with Carrot and Cabbage Slaw

SERVES 4 / PREP TIME: 10 MINUTES,
PLUS 20 MINUTES TO MARINATE
COOK TIME: 10 MINUTES

EQUIPMENT NEEDED: SPAGHETTI AND
RIBBON BLADES

This simple-to-prepare dish is incredibly delicious. The teriyaki sauce also works well with beef, fish, or a vegetarian protein of your choice. If you're trying to save on time, skip marinating the chicken and serve the carrot and cabbage slaw raw, tossed with the coconut aminos sauce.

⅓ cup coconut aminos

1 tablespoon sesame oil

1 teaspoon sea salt

1 tablespoon honey (optional)

1 tablespoon Asian hot sauce (optional)

1 pound boneless, skinless chicken breasts

1 tablespoon coconut oil

½-inch piece fresh ginger, grated

3 garlic cloves, minced

3 medium carrots, spiralized with the spaghetti blade

½ head green cabbage, spiralized with the ribbon blade

3 scallions, white and green parts, chopped

1. In a small bowl, mix the coconut aminos, sesame oil, salt, honey (if using), and hot sauce (if using). Put the chicken in a large glass dish or bowl and pour half of the marinade over it. Let marinate for 20 minutes. Reserve the other half of the marinade.

2. Heat the coconut oil in a large skillet over medium heat. Add the chicken and its marinade. Add the ginger and garlic. Let the chicken cook for about 5 minutes then flip the breasts. Continue cooking for about 5 minutes, stirring occasionally, until the marinade has thickened and the chicken has reached an internal temperature of at least 165°F.

3. Put the remaining reserved marinade, carrot noodles, and cabbage ribbons in a large pan over medium heat. Sauté for 3 to 5 minutes, stirring frequently, or until the vegetables reach the texture you prefer.

4. Divide the vegetables among four plates. Top with the chicken and sauce, and garnish with the scallions.

Cooking Tip: To make sure the chicken breasts cook evenly, pound them to an even thickness first. If you don't have a mallet, you can use the bottom of a Mason jar wrapped in plastic wrap.

Thai Lettuce Wraps with Pork

EQUIPMENT NEEDED: SPAGHETTI AND
RIBBON BLADES

I'm not going to lie: There are definitely days when I crave tortillas and bread. However, with these Thai Lettuce Wraps you won't even realize the tortilla is missing. These wraps combine a zesty slaw with flavorful homemade sausage, all wrapped up in lettuce. Sure, it's not a tortilla, but it's every bit as satisfying.

FOR THE SLAW

1 medium carrot, peeled, spiralized with the spaghetti blade

1 medium daikon radish, peeled, spiralized with the spaghetti blade

¼ red cabbage, spiralized with the ribbon blade

½ cup chopped fresh cilantro

Juice of 1 lime

FOR THE WRAPS

1 pound pastured ground pork

2 garlic cloves, minced

2 scallions, white and green parts, finely chopped

½-inch piece fresh ginger, grated

1 tablespoon freshly squeezed lime juice

1 teaspoon Asian hot sauce

½ teaspoon sea salt

1 tablespoon coconut oil

8 large romaine lettuce leaves

¼ cup chopped Thai basil leaves

1 lime, cut into wedges

Coconut aminos

To make the slaw

1. Combine the carrot and radish noodles, cabbage ribbons, cilantro, and lime juice in a large bowl. Mix well.

2. Set aside.

To make the wraps

1. Combine the pork, garlic, scallions, ginger, lime juice, hot sauce, and salt in a large mixing bowl. Mix until well incorporated. Divide the mixture into 8 (2-ounce) portions and use your hands to form them into patties.

2. Heat the coconut oil in a skillet over medium heat. Add the patties to the skillet in a single layer (cook in two batches if there's not enough room). Cook each side for 3 to 4 minutes, until the meat is golden brown and the internal temperature reaches at least 145°F.

3. When the sausage is cooked, lay the lettuce leaves out on four plates—two to a plate. Spoon some slaw onto each leaf, then top with a sausage patty and some basil.

4. Serve with the lime wedges, and coconut aminos for dipping.

Variation Tip: You can vary this recipe by serving the slaw on the side and filling the wraps with grilled jalapeño peppers, mung bean sprouts, and/or sliced avocado.

Weekend Pad Thai with Chicken

SERVES 4 / PREP TIME: 15 MINUTES
COOK TIME: 20 MINUTES

EQUIPMENT NEEDED: SPAGHETTI AND
RIBBON BLADES

*This pad thai is for all those nights (or week-
ends) where you decide to skip the never-ending
to-do list. It has all the flavors of your favorite
takeout, but none of the refined flour, sugars, or
preservatives. Vegetarian or vegan? No problem! Leave out the chicken and double the eggs.
Or leave out both and sub in tofu.*

1 tablespoon tamarind paste

2 tablespoons coconut aminos

2 tablespoons freshly squeezed lime juice

2 tablespoons sesame oil

5 garlic cloves, minced

1-inch piece fresh ginger, grated

2 tablespoons coconut oil, divided

1 pound boneless, skinless chicken thighs or breasts,
    cut into strips

4 eggs, lightly beaten

2 medium sweet potatoes, peeled, spiralized with
    the spaghetti blade

1 carrot, spiralized with the spaghetti blade

½ head cabbage, spiralized with the ribbon blade

2 cups bean sprouts

6 scallions, white and green parts, sliced

½ cup roasted cashews, chopped

1 lime, cut into wedges

1. Mix the tamarind paste, coconut aminos, lime juice, sesame oil, garlic, and ginger in a small bowl. Set aside.

2. Heat 1 tablespoon of the coconut oil in a medium skillet over medium heat. Add about 2 tablespoons of the tamarind sauce. Add the chicken and cook for 8 to 10 minutes, stirring occasionally. When the chicken has reached at least 165°F, remove from the heat.

3. While the chicken is cooking, heat the remaining 1 tablespoon of coconut oil in a large skillet over medium heat. Add the eggs, and scramble them in the pan for 1 or 2 minutes, until cooked.

4. Add the sweet potato, carrot, and cabbage noodles, and the remaining tamarind sauce to the eggs. Cook for 8 to 10 minutes, or until the vegetable noodles are tender.

5. Toss in the cooked chicken, bean sprouts, and scallions. Top with the cashews and serve with a wedge of lime.

Ingredient Tip: Tamarind paste is popular in many Asian dishes. It tastes slightly sweet and sour, as it comes from the sour fruit of tamarind trees. It can be found at any Asian market, as well as most health food stores and many grocery stores.

Slow Cooker Thai Beef Curry with Noodles

SERVES 6 / PREP TIME: 10 MINUTES
COOK TIME: 6 TO 8 HOURS

EQUIPMENT NEEDED: FETTUCCINE BLADE

There's nothing better than coming home to a hot meal after a long day at work, which is why my trusty slow cooker gets regular workouts. I set everything up in the slow cooker before I leave, and just cook the zucchini when I get home. Most Thai curry recipes call for kaffir lime leaves, but this ingredient can sometimes be hard to find. In this recipe, fresh lime zest is used instead to add brightness to the curry. If fresh lemongrass is not available, you can substitute 1 teaspoon of dried lemongrass or omit it entirely.

2 tablespoons coconut oil, divided

1 (1½-pound) boneless beef chuck roast, trimmed of excess fat

4 tablespoons Thai red curry paste

1 medium onion, chopped

1 (13.5-ounce) can full-fat unsweetened coconut milk

1 teaspoon sea salt

2 cups cremini mushrooms, chopped

1 medium red bell pepper, seeded and chopped

1 stalk fresh lemongrass, finely sliced

1 teaspoon ground cumin

6 medium zucchini, spiralized with the fettuccine blade

2 teaspoons freshly grated lime zest

½ cup chopped fresh Thai basil leaves or cilantro

1. Heat 1 tablespoon of the coconut oil in a medium skillet over medium-high heat. Add the meat, sear for 1 to 2 minutes, then flip and sear the other side. Place the meat in the slow cooker.

2. Add the curry paste and onion to the same skillet and cook, stirring frequently, until fragrant, about 30 seconds. Add the curry paste and onion to the slow cooker, along with the coconut milk, salt, mushrooms, bell pepper, lemongrass, and cumin.

3. Cook on low for 6 to 8 hours, or until the beef is tender.

4. Heat the remaining 1 tablespoon of coconut oil in a medium skillet over medium heat. Sauté the zoodles for 3 to 5 minutes, or until they are the texture you prefer. Drain any excess liquid from the pan.

5. Divide the zoodles among six bowls. Stir the lime zest into the curry and spoon the curry over the noodles. Garnish with the basil.

Cooking Tip: Browning the meat, onion, and curry paste before slow cooking will bring out the most flavor. However, if you are short on time, skip these steps and just add everything directly to the slow cooker.

Spicy Salmon over Cucumber Noodles

SERVES 4 / PREP TIME: 10 MINUTES, PLUS AT
LEAST 20 MINUTES TO MARINATE
COOK TIME: 10 MINUTES

EQUIPMENT NEEDED: RIBBON BLADE

Do you have to force yourself into eating fish?
If so, I promise that this spicy salmon will be a
complete game-changer, especially when paired
with these simple, fresh cucumber noodles.

5 garlic cloves, minced
¼ cup plus 2 tablespoons coconut aminos
3 tablespoons sesame oil
2 tablespoons honey (optional)
½ teaspoon paprika
2 to 3 tablespoons Asian hot sauce, or as desired
4 (6-ounce) wild salmon fillets
2 tablespoons coconut oil
2 medium cucumbers
1 medium red bell pepper, stemmed, spiralized with
    the ribbon blade, then seeded
Sea salt
Freshly ground black pepper
2 tablespoons sesame seeds (optional)

1. Put the garlic, coconut aminos, sesame oil, honey (if using), and paprika in a small bowl and mix well. Add the hot sauce until you reach the level of desired heat. Reserve ¼ cup of the sauce.

2. Place the salmon in a glass dish and top with the remaining sauce. Marinate in the refrigerator for at least 20 minutes and up to 6 hours, turning the fish at least once.

3. Heat the coconut oil in a large pan over medium-high heat. Add the salmon, along with any excess marinade from the dish.

4. Cook the salmon for about 5 minutes, turn over, and cook for 5 minutes, or until the internal temperature reaches 135°F.

5. While the salmon is cooking, spiralize the cucumbers with the ribbon blade and place on paper towels to absorb any excess liquid.

6. When the salmon is ready, toss the cucumber ribbons with the bell pepper noodles and a pinch of salt and pepper.

7. Divide the vegetables among four plates and top with the salmon, along with the reserved sauce. Garnish with the sesame seeds (if using).

Cooking Tip: Short on time? No problem! Skip marinating the salmon and this dish can be ready in as little as 15 minutes.

Cashew Chicken

SERVES 4 / PREP TIME: 15 MINUTES
COOK TIME: 15 MINUTES

EQUIPMENT NEEDED: SPAGHETTI AND
RIBBON BLADES

There is nothing I love more than Asian food, and this healthier version of Cashew Chicken is one of my absolute favorites! I usually enjoy it over cauliflower "rice" or a bed of fresh spinach.

2 tablespoons sesame oil

1 pound boneless, skinless chicken thighs or breasts, shredded

3 garlic cloves, minced

½-inch piece fresh ginger, grated

1 medium red bell pepper, stemmed, spiralized with the ribbon blade, then seeded

1 head broccoli, florets chopped into bite-size pieces and the stalk spiralized with the spaghetti blade

1 medium onion, chopped

⅓ cup coconut aminos

1 teaspoon arrowroot powder

½ teaspoon sea salt

¼ teaspoon crushed red pepper flakes

1 cup roasted whole cashews

3 scallions, white and green parts, chopped

1. Heat the sesame oil in a large skillet over medium heat. Add the chicken, garlic, and ginger. Let the chicken cook for about 7 minutes, stirring occasionally.

2. Add the bell pepper, broccoli, and onion, and cook for 5 minutes, stirring occasionally.

3. In a small bowl, mix the coconut aminos with the arrowroot powder, salt, and red pepper flakes. Add the coconut aminos mixture to the chicken and add the cashews. Cook for 1 to 2 minutes, stirring frequently, until the sauce has thickened. Check that the chicken is fully cooked and has reached an internal temperature of at least 165°F.

4. Remove from the heat. Add the scallions and serve warm.

Variation Tip: Not a fan of broccoli? Try subbing spiralized zucchini or chopped celery instead.

Chicken and Veggie Chow Mein

SERVES 4 / PREP TIME: 10 MINUTES
COOK TIME: 15 MINUTES

EQUIPMENT NEEDED: SPAGHETTI AND
RIBBON BLADES

Chow mein, which means "stir-fried noodles," is one of the most popular Chinese takeout dishes. With this healthy recipe, you can eat your noodle veggies while still satisfying your craving for an old standby.

2 tablespoons sesame oil, divided

1 pound boneless, skinless chicken thighs or breasts, cut into strips

1 tablespoon coconut oil

3 garlic cloves, minced

1-inch piece fresh ginger, grated

3 medium zucchini, spiralized with the spaghetti blade

2 medium carrots, peeled, spiralized with the spaghetti blade

½ head green cabbage, spiralized with the ribbon blade

5 celery stalks, thinly sliced

2 tablespoons coconut aminos

4 scallions, white and green parts, chopped

Sea salt

Freshly ground black pepper

1. Heat 1 tablespoon of the sesame oil in a medium pan over medium heat. Add the chicken and cook for 8 to 10 minutes, stirring occasionally. Make sure the chicken has reached at least 165°F, then remove from the heat.

2. While the chicken is cooking, put the remaining 1 tablespoon of sesame oil, coconut oil, garlic, and ginger in a large pan over medium-high heat. Sauté for 1 minute, until the ginger and garlic are fragrant.

3. Add the zucchini, carrot, and cabbage noodles, along with the celery, and cook, stirring frequently, for 3 to 5 minutes, until the noodles are just tender.

4. Drain any water from the pan and add the coconut aminos, scallions, and chicken.

5. Season with salt and pepper. Serve hot.

Make It Vegan: Leave out the chicken and sub in some sprouted tofu, tempeh, or edamame.

Beef and Green Bean Stir-Fry

SERVES 4 / PREP TIME: 10 MINUTES
COOK TIME: 15 MINUTES

EQUIPMENT NEEDED: SPAGHETTI BLADE

This dish is a go-to of mine because it's so simple (all you need is one large skillet!) and yet the results are always better than any takeout. I prefer daikon radish noodles in this recipe, since they are so like vermicelli in appearance and texture, but you can always substitute another vegetable if daikon is just not a favorite.

2 tablespoons coconut oil, divided

1 pound grass-fed sirloin beef, thinly sliced

1 pound green beans, trimmed and halved

1 large daikon radish, peeled, spiralized with the spaghetti blade

1 medium onion, sliced

3 garlic cloves, minced

½-inch piece fresh ginger, grated

½ teaspoon sea salt, plus more for final seasoning

¼ cup coconut aminos

1 tablespoon sesame oil

1 teaspoon arrowroot powder

Freshly ground black pepper

1. Heat 1 tablespoon of the coconut oil in a large skillet over medium heat. Add the beef and cook, stirring frequently, for 3 to 4 minutes, until it is browned. Set the beef aside, along with any cooking juices.

2. Add the remaining 1 tablespoon of coconut oil to the skillet, along with the green beans, daikon radish noodles, onion, garlic, and ginger. Sauté for 3 to 5 minutes, stirring occasionally, until the beans are crisp-tender and bright green.

3. Add the salt, coconut aminos, and sesame oil. Return the beef to the pan, along with any juices. Let it simmer for 5 minutes, stirring occasionally.

4. Tilt the pan to one side so the sauce collects in a pool. Whisk the arrowroot powder into the sauce and simmer for 1 to 2 minutes, until the sauce is thick. Straighten the pan and stir the sauce so the mixture is well coated.

5. Season with salt and pepper. Serve warm.

Cooking Tip: If you decide to substitute zucchini for the daikon, sauté the zoodles separately, drain them, then add them to the dish at the end.

Mongolian Beef over Cabbage

SERVES 4 / PREP TIME: 10 MINUTES
COOK TIME: 15 MINUTES

EQUIPMENT NEEDED: RIBBON BLADE

Mongolian Beef is a popular dish of flank steak tossed with a sugary brown sauce and served over fried cellophane noodles. I don't know about you, but that sounds like heaven to my taste buds, followed by a stomachache. Luckily, with this version, you can have it all—without the stomachache!

1 tablespoon sesame oil

1 pound flank steak, thinly sliced against the grain

½ medium onion, finely diced

½-inch piece fresh ginger, grated

3 garlic cloves, minced

½ teaspoon sea salt

¾ cup coconut aminos

2 teaspoons arrowroot powder

1 tablespoon coconut oil

1 small head (or ½ large) green cabbage, spiralized with the ribbon blade

3 scallions, white and green parts, chopped

1. Heat the sesame oil in a medium saucepan over medium heat. Add the flank steak, onion, ginger, and garlic, and sauté for 2 to 3 minutes, or until the garlic is fragrant. Add the salt and coconut aminos, and let simmer for 5 minutes.

2. When the steak has reached at least 145°F, whisk in the arrowroot powder and let simmer for 1 to 2 minutes, until the sauce is thick. Set aside.

3. Heat the coconut oil in a medium pan over medium heat, and add the cabbage ribbons. Cook, stirring frequently, for 7 to 10 minutes, until the cabbage ribbons reach the texture you prefer.

4. Divide the cabbage ribbons among four plates and top with the beef and scallions.

Variation Tip: Craving something spicy? Try adding ½ teaspoon (or more) of red pepper flakes to the sauce along with the coconut aminos in step 1.

Green Vegetable Curry over Zucchini Noodles

VEGAN

SERVES 4 / PREP TIME: 5 MINUTES
COOK TIME: 15 MINUTES

EQUIPMENT NEEDED: FETTUCCINE BLADE

With minimal prep and cooking time, this dish is truly an easy weeknight meal. Thai green curry paste is a blend of chiles and herbs and has a bit more heat than red curry paste. It can be found at any Asian market, as well as most health food stores and many grocery stores. Some brands contain shrimp, so be sure to check the ingredient list if that's a concern. This curry is versatile, so feel free to substitute other vegetables or add in a protein of your choice to make it even more filling.

2 tablespoons coconut oil, divided
4 tablespoons Thai green curry paste
4 cups broccoli florets
4 baby bok choy, chopped
1 medium red bell pepper, seeded, chopped into
    1-inch pieces
1 (13.5-ounce) can full-fat unsweetened coconut milk
4 medium zucchini, spiralized with the fettuccine blade
½ cup fresh basil leaves

1. Heat 1 tablespoon of the coconut oil in a large pan over medium-high heat. Add the curry paste and cook, stirring frequently, for about 30 seconds, until fragrant. Add the broccoli, bok choy, and bell pepper, and cook, stirring frequently, for about 5 minutes, until the broccoli is bright green and crisp tender.

2. Add the coconut milk and bring just to a simmer. Reduce the heat and cook until the vegetables are tender, 8 to 10 minutes.

3. While the curry is cooking, heat the remaining 1 tablespoon of coconut oil in another pan over medium heat. Add the zoodles and cook for 2 to 3 minutes, until just tender. Drain and set aside.

4. When the curry is finished cooking, divide the zoodles among four bowls. Top with the curry and basil leaves.

Ingredient Tip: I always keep a jar of Thai curry paste handy, but if you don't plan to use it up within two weeks, freeze the leftover paste in small portions in an airtight container, so it stays fresh and can be defrosted as you need it.

Coconut-Lime Broccoli Stir-Fry

VEGETARIAN

SERVES 4 / PREP TIME: 10 MINUTES
COOK TIME: 10 MINUTES

EQUIPMENT NEEDED: SPAGHETTI BLADE

This slightly sweet and tart stir-fry is the perfect balance of fresh veggies and comfort food flavor. This is one of my favorite winter dishes on a cold day, and it goes well with any protein source of your choice. Celeriac is a variety of celery grown for its knobby root. It tastes like a subtle blend of parsley and celery.

1 tablespoon coconut oil

1 head broccoli, florets chopped into bite-size pieces, stalk spiralized with the spaghetti blade

2 large celeriac roots, peeled, spiralized with the spaghetti blade

1 cup full-fat unsweetened canned coconut milk

Zest and juice of 1 lime

2 tablespoons coconut aminos

2 tablespoons honey or maple syrup

½ teaspoon sea salt

2 teaspoons arrowroot powder

1. Heat the coconut oil in a large skillet over medium heat. Add the broccoli and celeriac noodles and cook, stirring frequently, for about 5 minutes, until the broccoli is bright green and crisp-tender.

2. Mix the coconut milk, lime zest and juice, coconut aminos, honey, and salt in a medium bowl. Whisk in the arrowroot powder.

3. Add the sauce to the vegetables and cook for 1 to 2 minutes, stirring frequently, until the sauce has thickened and the broccoli and noodles have reached the texture you prefer. Serve warm.

Substitution Tip: Celeriac is a winter vegetable and can be hard to find out of season. Feel free to substitute parsnips, daikon radish, or zucchini instead.

Chicken Coconut Curry

SERVES 4 / PREP TIME: 10 MINUTES
COOK TIME: 40 MINUTES

EQUIPMENT NEEDED: SPAGHETTI BLADE

Not only is this curry full of healthy fats and protein, but the spices are also loaded with anti-inflammatory properties. Whether you're trying to recover from a tough workout or a long day, this recipe fits the bill! The flavor base is garam masala, a blend of eight or more spices. Find it in supermarkets, health food stores, and Indian and Asian grocery stores.

2 tablespoons coconut oil, divided

1 pound boneless, skinless chicken thighs, cut into bite-size pieces

1 medium onion, finely diced

3 garlic cloves, minced

2-inch cinnamon stick

2 bay leaves

1-inch piece fresh ginger, grated

1 teaspoon ground cumin

1 teaspoon garam masala

1 teaspoon ground turmeric

1 (13.5-ounce) can full-fat unsweetened coconut milk

2 tablespoons tomato paste

1 teaspoon sea salt

5 cups broccoli florets

3 medium carrots, peeled, spiralized with the spaghetti blade

4 medium zucchini, spiralized with the spaghetti blade

½ cup chopped fresh cilantro

1. Heat 1 tablespoon of the coconut oil in a medium pot over medium heat. Add the chicken and cook for about 5 minutes, stirring frequently.

2. Add the onion, garlic, cinnamon stick, bay leaves, ginger, cumin, garam masala, and turmeric. Cook for 1 minute, until the spices are fragrant.

3. Add the coconut milk, tomato paste, and salt. Bring to a boil then reduce the heat and simmer, covered, for about 20 minutes. Add the broccoli and carrot noodles and cook for 5 to 10 minutes, until the vegetables are just tender.

4. While the curry is cooking, heat the remaining 1 tablespoon of coconut oil in another pan over medium heat. Add the zucchini noodles and cook for 2 to 3 minutes, until just tender. Drain and set aside.

5. When the curry is finished cooking, divide the zucchini noodles among four bowls. Top with the curry and cilantro.

Make It Vegan: Substitute 2 cups of a protein source of choice (such as sprouted tofu or legumes) instead of the chicken.

Jalapeño-Sesame Salmon Stir-Fry

SERVES 4 / PREP TIME: 10 MINUTES
COOK TIME: 15 MINUTES

EQUIPMENT NEEDED: SPAGHETTI AND
RIBBON BLADES

I wasn't always a fan of spicy dishes, but in 2015 I took a trip to Arizona and every local dish I tried had some form of spicy pepper in it. I finally became hooked! When I returned home, I started adding jalapeño peppers to omelets, curries, soups, and even this salmon stir-fry. If you're not a fan of spicy foods, feel free to leave the jalapeño out, or remove the seeds to lessen the heat.

3 tablespoons coconut oil

3 tablespoons sesame oil

2 tablespoons coconut aminos

2 tablespoons freshly squeezed lime juice

1 tablespoon honey

2 garlic cloves, minced

1-inch piece fresh ginger, grated

½ teaspoon sea salt

4 (4- to 6-ounce) salmon fillets

1 jalapeño pepper, sliced, plus more for serving

1 medium red bell pepper, stemmed, spiralized with the ribbon blade, then seeded

3 medium zucchini, spiralized with the ribbon blade

1 medium carrot, peeled, spiralized with the spaghetti blade

½ onion, spiralized with the ribbon blade

1. Put the coconut oil, sesame oil, coconut aminos, lime juice, honey, garlic, ginger, and salt in a small bowl and mix.

2. Heat half of the sesame dressing in a large skillet over medium-high heat. Add the salmon and the jalapeño slices.

3. Cook the salmon for about 5 minutes, turn over and cook for 5 minutes, or until the internal temperature reaches 135°F.

4. In another large pan over medium-high heat, add about 1 tablespoon of the sesame dressing along with the bell pepper, zucchini, carrot, and onion noodles. Sauté for 3 to 5 minutes, or until the vegetables reach the texture you prefer.

5. Remove from the heat and drain any excess liquid. Toss with the remaining sesame dressing. Divide among four plates and top with the salmon and jalapeños.

Variation Tip: One of the best things about a stir-fry is that it's extremely versatile. If you don't have the specific vegetables listed in this recipe, no problem! Sub in other veggies of your choice.

Citrus-Ginger Glazed White Fish

SERVES 4 / PREP TIME: 10 MINUTES
COOK TIME: 15 MINUTES

EQUIPMENT NEEDED: SPAGHETTI BLADE

This is one of my favorite dinners in early autumn, when the body starts craving heartier dishes. The white fish goes well with this citrus-ginger sauce, but you can also substitute chicken for a healthier version of traditional orange chicken.

½ cup orange juice

1 tablespoon apple cider vinegar

3 garlic cloves, minced

½-inch piece fresh ginger, grated

2 tablespoons sesame oil

1 teaspoon ground cumin

½ teaspoon sea salt, plus a pinch, plus more for final seasoning

4 (4- to 6-ounce) white fish fillets, such as cod or halibut

1 tablespoon coconut oil

1 large butternut squash, bulbous end removed, upper part peeled, then spiralized with the spaghetti blade

Pinch freshly ground black pepper, plus more for final seasoning

2 tablespoons white sesame seeds

1. In a large skillet, combine the orange juice, apple cider vinegar, garlic, ginger, sesame oil, cumin, and salt. Bring the sauce to a boil, lower the heat, and simmer for 5 minutes, or until the sauce is slightly thickened. Add the fish to the skillet and cook for about 5 minutes, then flip. Cook for 5 minutes, or until the internal temperature reaches 135°F.

2. Heat the coconut oil in another large skillet over medium heat. And the butternut squash noodles, season with a pinch of salt and pepper, and cook for 8 to 10 minutes, stirring frequently, or until the noodles are tender.

3. Divide the butternut squash noodles among four plates and top with the fish, along with any cooking juices.

4. Garnish with the sesame seeds and season with salt and pepper. Serve hot.

Ingredient Tip: One of my favorite ways to cook the squash from the bulbous end is to peel and dice it, toss it with a bit of coconut oil, salt, and cinnamon, then roast in a 400°F oven for 20 minutes, or until the squash is tender.

Fish Taco Wraps with Avocado Dressing

SERVES 4 / PREP TIME: 15 MINUTES
COOK TIME: 10 MINUTES

EQUIPMENT NEEDED: SPAGHETTI AND
RIBBON BLADES

These take me back to the summer of 2013. That was the year I discovered fish tacos, and dangerously enough, there was the best *taco truck that I'd pass every day on my way home from working out. Looking back, I still don't know how I survived those intense workouts. But with the promise of fish tacos after, I never missed a class.*

FOR THE AVOCADO DRESSING

1 medium ripe avocado, pitted
¼ cup chopped fresh cilantro
¼ cup freshly squeezed lime juice
2 tablespoons extra-virgin olive oil
½ teaspoon ground cumin
½ teaspoon garlic powder
¼ teaspoon sea salt

FOR THE SLAW

1 medium jicama, peeled, spiralized with the
    spaghetti blade
¼ red cabbage, spiralized with the ribbon blade
½ cup chopped fresh cilantro
Juice of 1 lime

FOR THE FISH

1½ teaspoons smoked paprika
½ teaspoon chili powder
½ teaspoon ground cumin
½ teaspoon salt
1 tablespoon coconut oil
4 (4- to 6-ounce) white fish fillets, such as cod
    or halibut
1 garlic clove, minced
8 large romaine lettuce leaves
1 lime, cut into wedges

To make the avocado dressing

1. Add the avocado, cilantro, lime juice, olive oil, cumin, garlic powder, and salt to a blender. Blend until smooth.

2. Set aside for the flavors to meld.

To make the slaw

1. In a large bowl, combine the jicama noodles, red cabbage ribbons, cilantro, and lime juice. Mix well.

2. Set aside.

To make the fish

1. Mix the paprika, chili powder, cumin, and salt together in a small bowl. Sprinkle it over the fish and rub it in well.

2. Heat the coconut oil in a large skillet over medium-high heat. Add the fish and garlic and cook for about 5 minutes, then flip. Cook for 5 minutes, or until the internal temperature of the fish reaches 135°F.

3. When the fish is cooked, lay the lettuce leaves out, two to a plate. Cut each fish fillet in half and put a piece of fish on each lettuce leaf. Top with slaw and avocado dressing.

4. Serve with the lime wedges and any extra slaw and dressing on the side.

Variation Tip: Craving a spicier taco wrap? Cook the fish with sliced jalapeño peppers or add a bit of diced jalapeño to the dressing before blending.

5

Light and Lovely Salads

Summer Fruit Salad with Honey-Lime Vinaigrette

SERVES 4 / PREP TIME: 10 MINUTES

EQUIPMENT NEEDED: SPAGHETTI BLADE

Before we get to the vegetables, let's start with a fruit salad. This is a beautiful, refreshing dessert for the summertime. Serve in chilled martini glasses for a fun presentation.

2 tablespoons honey

1 tablespoon freshly squeezed lime juice

1 teaspoon freshly grated lime zest

½ medium jicama, peeled, spiralized with the spaghetti blade

1 pint fresh blueberries

1 pint fresh raspberries

1 pint fresh strawberries, hulled and quartered

2 tablespoons chopped fresh mint leaves

1. Mix the honey, lime juice, and lime zest together in a small bowl until well combined. Set aside.

2. In a large bowl, toss the jicama, blueberries, raspberries, and strawberries. Add the honey-lime vinaigrette and toss to combine.

3. Sprinkle with the chopped mint and refrigerate until serving.

Variation Tip: You can use any seasonal fruit in this salad. Try local melon, peaches, or nectarines in place of the berries.

Early Spring Salad

VEGAN

SERVES 2 TO 4 / PREP TIME: 10 MINUTES
COOK TIME: 5 MINUTES

EQUIPMENT NEEDED: SPAGHETTI BLADE

This is one of my favorite salads for the beginning of spring, when there are just a few hints of green produce popping up at the market. Pea shoots have a delicate and sweet flavor that is a perfect addition. But if you can't find them, feel free to substitute sprouts, watercress, baby spinach, thinly sliced asparagus, or other seasonal vegetables. Pair this salad with a bowl of warm soup for a light lunch on a chilly spring day.

¼ cup pine nuts

1 large fennel bulb, green stems removed, spiralized with the spaghetti blade

4 celery stalks, thinly sliced

1 bunch red radishes, tops trimmed, sliced

2 cups pea shoots

3 tablespoons freshly squeezed lemon juice

3 tablespoons extra-virgin olive oil

Sea salt

Freshly ground black pepper

1. Put the pine nuts in a dry skillet over medium-low heat. Heat for about 3 minutes, stirring frequently, or until they're just golden brown. Remove from the heat.

2. Toss the fennel, celery, radishes, pea shoots, lemon juice, and olive oil together in a large bowl.

3. Season with salt and pepper and serve, topped with the toasted pine nuts.

Ingredient Tip: Pea shoots have traditionally been popular in Asian cuisine, but they're popping up in more farmers' markets and health food stores, since they're nutritionally dense and can be harvested quickly. They're in season in early and mid-spring. Look for pea shoots that are fresh and bright green, without any bruises or discoloration.

Light and Crunchy Kohlrabi Slaw

SERVES 4 / PREP TIME: 5 MINUTES

EQUIPMENT NEEDED: SPAGHETTI BLADE

Have you ever eaten kohlrabi? Many years ago when I was a food educator working with children and families, I'd get blank stares when I brought up kohlrabi. It was pretty clear that kohlrabi was the alien of the root vegetable family. Kohlrabi is typically in season fall through spring and has a slightly sweet flavor, similar to a broccoli stalk. In this salad it pairs well with a simple dressing and a tart apple. If you have a bit of extra time, try topping this salad with roasted pumpkin seeds or pistachios for extra crunch and flavor.

2 medium kohlrabi, peeled, spiralized with the spaghetti blade

1 medium Granny Smith apple, spiralized with the spaghetti blade

3 tablespoons extra-virgin olive oil

1 tablespoon apple cider vinegar

1 tablespoon brown mustard

Sea salt

Freshly ground black pepper

1. Place the kohlrabi and apple noodles, olive oil, apple cider vinegar, and mustard in a large bowl and toss to combine.

2. Season with salt and pepper. Serve immediately or refrigerate and serve later.

Substitution Tip: Is kohlrabi out of season or hard to find? Substitute three or four medium broccoli stalks or one medium daikon radish instead.

Zucchini Caprese

VEGAN

SERVES 4 / PREP TIME: 10 MINUTES

EQUIPMENT NEEDED: SPAGHETTI BLADE

Is there anything better than fresh tomatoes and basil? With this incredible homemade cashew "cheese," you won't even miss the mozzarella!

½ cup whole raw cashews
2 tablespoons extra-virgin olive oil, divided
1 tablespoon nutritional yeast
½ teaspoon garlic powder
½ teaspoon sea salt, plus more for final seasoning
4 medium zucchini, spiralized with the spaghetti blade
2 cups cherry tomatoes, halved
½ cup fresh basil leaves, cut into chiffonade
Freshly ground black pepper

1. Put the cashews, 1 tablespoon of the olive oil, nutritional yeast, garlic powder, and salt in a food processor. Process, scraping down the sides as necessary, until the cashews form a smooth paste.

2. Toss the zoodles with the tomatoes, basil, and the remaining 1 tablespoon of olive oil.

3. Season with salt and pepper, crumble the cashew cheese over the salad, and serve cold.

Variation Tip: No food processor? Unfortunately, since there's very little liquid added, you can't make the cashew cheese in a blender. Instead, try lightly toasting and salting the cashews, then sprinkling them over the salad instead.

Lightened-Up Potato Salad

SERVES 4 / PREP TIME: 5 MINUTES
COOK TIME: 10 MINUTES

EQUIPMENT NEEDED: SPAGHETTI BLADE

At least once a year, I'll find myself panicking about what to bring to a potluck or picnic. In a situation like this, you have to go with potato salad. This recipe is a go-to because it's quick to prepare. Make it your own by adding fresh spinach, chopped bacon, or caramelize the onions. Just please, hold the mayo!

1 tablespoon coconut oil

2 medium sweet potatoes, peeled, spiralized with the spaghetti blade

2 garlic cloves, minced

3 scallions, white and green parts, finely diced

2 tablespoons extra-virgin olive oil

⅓ cup chopped fresh Italian (flat-leaf) parsley

3 tablespoons freshly squeezed lemon juice

2 tablespoons brown mustard

½ teaspoon sea salt

Freshly ground black pepper

1. Heat the coconut oil in a medium skillet over medium heat. Add the sweet potato noodles and garlic, and cook, stirring frequently to keep the noodles from sticking, 8 to 10 minutes, or until the noodles are cooked.

2. Toss with the scallions, olive oil, parsley, lemon juice, mustard, and salt. Season with black pepper.

3. Enjoy warm or store in the refrigerator to cool before serving.

Variation Tip: I opted for sweet potatoes in this version, but you can substitute russet potatoes if you're not eating Paleo. If you need to lower the carbs, use just one potato and add 4 cups of chopped romaine lettuce or dark, leafy greens. The salad will still have a satisfying flavor and texture.

Arugula and Herb Greek Salad

SERVES 4 / PREP TIME: 15 MINUTES

EQUIPMENT NEEDED: SPAGHETTI AND RIBBON BLADES

Most Greek salads rely on feta cheese for flavor, but you certainly won't miss it in this version. This Greek salad is loaded with a variety of fresh, colorful vegetables, tossed with a tangy herb dressing for an extra pop of flavor. It pairs well with grilled chicken for a complete meal.

FOR THE DRESSING

⅓ cup chopped fresh Italian (flat-leaf) parsley
¼ cup finely chopped fresh mint leaves
¼ cup extra-virgin olive oil
3 tablespoons red wine vinegar
1 garlic clove, minced
½ teaspoon dried basil
½ teaspoon dried oregano
Sea salt
Freshly ground black pepper

FOR THE SALAD

2 medium cucumbers, spiralized with the spaghetti blade
½ red onion, spiralized with the spaghetti blade
1 medium red bell pepper, stemmed, spiralized with the ribbon blade, then seeded
4 cups baby arugula
1 cup cherry tomatoes, halved
½ cup pitted Kalamata olives, halved

To make the dressing

In a medium bowl, whisk together all the dressing ingredients. Season with salt and pepper.

To make the salad

1. Place the cucumber and onion noodles, bell pepper ribbons, arugula, tomatoes, and olives in a large bowl, and toss to combine.

2. Drizzle the dressing over the salad and mix well. Divide among four plates and serve.

Cooking Tip: This salad keeps well, so make a double batch and pack some away in glass storage containers in the refrigerator, for easy grab-and-go lunches.

Creamy Dill Cucumber Salad

SERVES 4 / PREP TIME: 10 MINUTES

EQUIPMENT NEEDED: SPAGHETTI BLADE

I like to think of this as a "simple Sunday salad"—one of those salads that just comes together easily, but doesn't require any prior forethought or planning. It's a great way to use up produce that's been sitting around in your fridge and needs to be eaten, or to show off fresh, ripe produce at its peak that you just picked up at the market.

FOR THE DRESSING

½ cup raw cashews
⅓ cup plus 2 tablespoons water
1 garlic clove
½ teaspoon sea salt
2 tablespoons minced fresh dill leaves
2 tablespoons freshly squeezed lemon juice

FOR THE SALAD

2 large cucumbers, spiralized with the spaghetti blade
1 head romaine lettuce, chopped
¼ medium red onion, spiralized with the spaghetti blade
2 Roma tomatoes, chopped
Freshly ground black pepper

To make the dressing

1. Put all the ingredients for the dressing in a food processor. Process until smooth.

To make the salad

1. Toss the cucumber noodles, romaine, onion noodles, and tomatoes with the dressing.

2. Divide among four plates, season with black pepper, and serve immediately.

 Cooking Tip: Pair this salad with a protein of choice or a simple soup for a complete meal.

Fall Harvest Salad with Toasted Pecans

VEGAN

SERVES 4 / PREP TIME: 10 MINUTES
COOK TIME: 15 MINUTES

EQUIPMENT NEEDED: SPAGHETTI BLADE

Ripe pears might just be the best thing about fall. Am I right? This fall harvest salad combines fresh greens with a homemade pear vinaigrette and rosemary-toasted pecans for a truly decadent fall treat.

FOR THE VINAIGRETTE

1 Anjou pear, cored and diced
2 teaspoons brown mustard
2 tablespoons red wine vinegar
¼ cup extra-virgin olive oil

FOR THE SALAD

½ cup whole raw pecans
1 tablespoon coconut oil
1 teaspoon dried rosemary, crushed
½ teaspoon sea salt
8 cups baby spinach
2 Anjou pears, tops removed, spiralized with the spaghetti blade

Preheat the oven to 175°F.

To make the vinaigrette

Put the pear, mustard, and vinegar in a food processor or blender. With the blade running, add the olive oil in a thin stream. Process until smooth. Set aside.

To make the salad

1. Toss the pecans with the coconut oil, rosemary, and salt. Lay them flat on a baking sheet and bake, stirring occasionally, for 15 to 20 minutes, or until the nuts are lightly toasted.

2. Toss the spinach with the spiralized pears and vinaigrette.

3. Top with the toasted pecans and serve.

Ingredient Tip: The best way to preserve the healthy fats in nuts is to eat them raw or roast them at a low temperature (usually below 200°F). If you're short on time, the pecans can be added raw to this salad.

Warm Winter Squash with Tangy Dressing

SERVES 4 / PREP TIME: 10 MINUTES
COOK TIME: 10 MINUTES

EQUIPMENT NEEDED: SPAGHETTI AND
RIBBON BLADES

*I love salads, but living in the cool and rainy
Pacific Northwest, I find myself avoiding them
when fall rolls around. The solution? A warm
salad! This salad combines roasted butternut
squash with sweet onions, fresh greens, pomegranate seeds, and sliced almonds, plus a tangy
dressing. It's the perfect way to enjoy a salad on
a cool winter day.*

FOR THE DRESSING

¼ cup extra-virgin olive oil
2 tablespoons apple cider vinegar
1 tablespoon yellow mustard
Sea salt
Freshly ground black pepper

FOR THE SALAD

*1 large butternut squash, bulbous end cut off,
    top section peeled then spiralized with the
    spaghetti blade*
*1 medium onion, peeled, spiralized with
    the ribbon blade*
1 tablespoon coconut oil
6 cups baby arugula or kale
1 cup pomegranate seeds
⅓ cup sliced almonds

Preheat the oven to 375°F.

To make the dressing

In a small bowl, whisk together the olive oil,
vinegar, and mustard. Season with salt and
pepper. Set aside.

To make the salad

1. Toss the butternut squash and onion
noodles with the coconut oil and lay them flat
on a baking sheet. Roast for 10 to 15 minutes,
until the vegetables are tender.

2. Toss the roasted noodles with the arugula
and dressing.

3. Top with the pomegranate seeds and
almonds. Serve immediately.

Variation Tip: Instead of butternut squash, try
2 sweet potatoes or root vegetables of your
choice (parsnips, carrots, etc.).

Antipasto Salad

SERVES 4 / PREP TIME: 15 MINUTES

EQUIPMENT NEEDED: SPAGHETTI BLADE

My spiralizer and I are like BFFs on most days. This is especially true on days I make this salad. Pair this with Weeknight Minestrone (page 119) or Parsnip and Kale Zuppa Toscana (page 118) for a complete meal.

FOR THE DRESSING

3 tablespoons extra-virgin olive oil
2 tablespoons red wine vinegar
1 tablespoon freshly squeezed lemon juice
Sea salt
Freshly ground black pepper

FOR THE SALAD

2 medium zucchini, spiralized with the
    spaghetti blade
1 medium summer squash, spiralized with the
    spaghetti blade
1 large carrot, peeled, spiralized with the
    spaghetti blade
1 cup chopped artichoke hearts
1 cup finely chopped broccoli florets
1 Roma tomato, chopped
½ cup roasted red bell peppers
½ cup Kalamata olives, pitted and chopped
½ red onion, spiralized with the spaghetti blade

To make the dressing

Mix the olive oil, vinegar, and lemon juice in a small bowl. Season with salt and pepper and set aside.

To make the salad

1. Mix all the salad ingredients in a large bowl. Toss with the dressing.

2. Serve immediately or refrigerate until you're ready to serve.

 Variation Tip: For a non-vegan version of this salad, add 1 cup of cubed salami or pepperoni.

Kale and Lime Caesar

VEGETARIAN

SERVES 4 / PREP TIME: 10 MINUTES

EQUIPMENT NEEDED: RIBBON BLADE

I love Caesar salads. Except that I can't eat the croutons. And actually, I don't really like the taste of anchovies in the dressing, so usually I opt for a vegan version. And I have to avoid the cheese. This Kale and Lime Caesar is completely free of the usual gluten and dairy—and the anchovies—but still has all of the flavor. My favorite part is the jicama in place of croutons for a delightful crunch!

FOR THE DRESSING

½ cup raw cashews

⅓ cup plus 2 tablespoons water

¼ cup freshly squeezed lime juice

2 tablespoons nutritional yeast flakes

1 tablespoon brown mustard

1 teaspoon garlic powder

½ teaspoon honey or maple syrup (optional)

¼ teaspoon sea salt

FOR THE SALAD

4 cups baby kale

1 head romaine lettuce, chopped

½ medium jicama, peeled, spiralized with the
    ribbon blade

1 cup cherry tomatoes, halved

To make the dressing

Put all the dressing ingredients in a food processor or blender. Process until smooth. Set aside.

To make the salad

1. Toss the baby kale and romaine with the dressing.

2. Divide among four plates and top with the jicama ribbons and tomatoes. Serve immediately.

Ingredient Tip: Jicama is a juicy white root vegetable with a thick brown skin that's native to Mexico. Jicama is typically enjoyed raw and tastes like a savory version of an apple. It can be found in Latin American and Asian markets, and many health food and grocery stores. If you can't find it, substitute a crisp apple or carrot for a nice crunch and a boost of color.

Avocado and Tuna Salad

SERVES 2 TO 4 / PREP TIME: 10 MINUTES

EQUIPMENT NEEDED: RIBBON BLADE

Tuna has high levels of omega-3 fatty acids, making it a wonderful choice for a quick, healthy meal. I love combining it with a fresh avocado, along with some lemon juice and mustard for a delicious and completely mayo-free tuna salad.

1 avocado, pitted

3 tablespoons brown mustard

3 tablespoons freshly squeezed lemon juice

2 (5-ounce) cans tuna, drained

3 celery stalks, finely diced

2 scallions, white and green parts, finely diced

½ medium red bell pepper, stemmed, spiralized with the ribbon blade, then seeded

¼ medium red onion, spiralized with the ribbon blade

¼ cup chopped fresh Italian (flat-leaf) parsley

Sea salt

Freshly ground black pepper

4 cups chopped romaine lettuce

1. Put the avocado in a large bowl and mash with the mustard and lemon juice until well combined.

2. Mix in the tuna, celery, scallions, bell pepper and red onion ribbons, and parsley. Season with salt and pepper.

3. Serve the tuna salad on top of the bed of romaine.

Variation Tip: This tuna salad is also fabulous when served as a wrap, using fresh romaine leaves, kale, or collard greens.

Red Cabbage and Broccoli Slaw with Salmon and Orange-Sesame Dressing

This salad combines crunchy cabbage and broccoli with a fresh orange-sesame dressing and salmon, making it full of fiber, protein, and healthy omega-3 fatty acids. It's one of my favorite go-to recipes on a busy weeknight.

FOR THE DRESSING

3 tablespoons coconut aminos
3 tablespoons orange juice
3 tablespoons sesame oil
1 garlic clove, minced
½-inch piece fresh ginger, grated

FOR THE SALAD

1 tablespoon coconut oil
4 (6-ounce) wild salmon fillets
Sea salt
Freshly ground black pepper
1 head broccoli, florets chopped, stem peeled
    and spiralized with the spaghetti blade
1 small head red cabbage, spiralized with the
    ribbon blade
3 scallions, white and green parts, sliced
¼ cup chopped fresh cilantro

To make the dressing

Whisk together all the dressing ingredients in a small bowl. Set aside.

To make the salad

1. Heat the coconut oil in a medium skillet over medium heat. Season the salmon with salt and pepper and add to the skillet. Cook the salmon for about 5 minutes. Turn over and cook for 5 minutes, or until the internal temperature reaches 135°F.

2. Mix the broccoli, cabbage, scallions, and cilantro in a large bowl. Reserve about 2 tablespoons of the dressing, and toss the rest with the vegetables. Mix well.

3. Divide the salad among four plates. Top with the cooked salmon, and drizzle the remaining dressing over the salmon.

4. Season with salt and pepper and enjoy warm.

Substitution Tip: If you're not a fan of broccoli, try subbing two medium kohlrabi. Kohlrabi has a mild and sweet flavor, similar to a broccoli stalk, and pairs well with the cabbage in this salad.

Roasted Beet and Cherry Salad with Salmon

SERVES 4 / PREP TIME: 15 MINUTES
COOK TIME: 15 MINUTES

EQUIPMENT NEEDED: SPAGHETTI BLADE

Do you ever get in a salad rut? This version combines spicy arugula, sweet cherries, and sweet roasted beets with a tangy vinaigrette, served with a piece of wild salmon. It's definitely my cure for boring salad syndrome.

FOR THE VINAIGRETTE

¼ cup extra-virgin olive oil

¼ cup red wine vinegar

2 tablespoons balsamic vinegar

2 teaspoons brown mustard

½ teaspoon dried basil

½ teaspoon dried oregano

¼ teaspoon sea salt

Freshly ground black pepper

FOR THE SALAD

2 medium beets, peeled, spiralized with the
  spaghetti blade

2 tablespoons coconut oil, divided

4 (6-ounce) wild salmon fillets

Sea salt

Freshly ground black pepper

6 cups arugula

1 cup Bing cherries, pitted and sliced

Preheat the oven to 350°F.

To make the vinaigrette

In a medium bowl, whisk together the olive oil, red wine vinegar, balsamic vinegar, mustard, basil, oregano, and salt. Season with black pepper and set aside.

To make the salad

1. Toss the beets with 1 tablespoon of the coconut oil. Spread in an even layer on a baking sheet and roast for about 15 minutes, or until the beets are tender but not dry.

2. While the beets are roasting, heat the remaining 1 tablespoon of coconut oil in a medium skillet over medium heat. Season the salmon with salt and pepper and add to the skillet. Cook the salmon for about 5 minutes. Turn over and cook for 5 minutes, or until the internal temperature reaches 135°F.

3. Toss the roasted beets with the arugula and cherries. Pour the dressing over the vegetables and toss again.

4. Divide the salad among four plates and top with the salmon.

Cooking Tip: Too hot to turn on the oven? Enjoy the beets raw!

Summer Salad with Grilled Chicken

SERVES 4 / PREP TIME: 15 MINUTES
COOK TIME: 15 MINUTES

EQUIPMENT NEEDED: RIBBON BLADE

There are a few key things that make a salad interesting: appearance, texture, and flavor. This colorful salad combines the crunchiness of raw summer vegetables with the sweetness of fresh blueberries and tomatoes, and a simple mix of balsamic vinegar and olive oil, for a delicious summer meal.

1 pound skinless, boneless chicken breasts

1 tablespoon safflower oil

Sea salt

Freshly ground black pepper

¼ cup balsamic vinegar

¼ cup extra-virgin olive oil

¼ cup fresh basil leaves, cut into chiffonade

2 medium summer squash, spiralized with the ribbon blade

1 medium red bell pepper, stemmed, spiralized with the ribbon blade, then seeded

1 medium zucchini, spiralized with the ribbon blade

½ medium red onion, spiralized with the ribbon blade

2 cups cherry tomatoes, sliced

1 cup blueberries

1. Preheat the grill.

2. Brush the chicken with the safflower oil and season with salt and pepper. Grill the chicken on both sides, 5 to 7 minutes per side, or until the internal temperature reaches 165°F. Set aside.

3. Whisk together the vinegar, olive oil, and basil in a large bowl. Add the summer squash, bell pepper, zucchini, and red onion ribbons. Toss well, until all the vegetables are coated.

4. Divide among four plates and top with the grilled chicken, tomatoes, and blueberries. Season with salt and pepper.

Cooking Tip: If you don't have a grill, you can also cook the chicken in a skillet on the stove top. Follow the directions for cooking chicken breasts in Asian-Style Cobb Salad (page 100).

Strawberry and Avocado Salad with Grilled Chicken

SERVES 4 / PREP TIME: 15 MINUTES
COOK TIME: 10 MINUTES

EQUIPMENT NEEDED: RIBBON BLADE

Is there anything better than the combination of fresh, ripe strawberries and grilled chicken in a salad? If you don't have a grill, you can also cook the chicken in a skillet on the stove top. Follow the directions for cooking chicken breasts in Asian-Style Cobb Salad (page 100).

FOR THE DRESSING

¼ cup extra-virgin olive oil
3 tablespoons apple cider vinegar
1 tablespoon honey or maple syrup
Sea salt
Freshly ground black pepper

FOR THE SALAD

1 pound boneless, skinless chicken breasts
1 tablespoon safflower oil
Sea salt
Freshly ground black pepper
8 cups baby spinach
1 medium cucumber, spiralized with the ribbon blade
1 medium shallot, finely diced
1 medium avocado, pitted and sliced
1 pint strawberries, sliced
¼ cup walnuts, chopped

Preheat the grill.

To make the dressing

In a medium bowl, whisk together all the ingredients for the dressing. Set aside.

To make the salad

1. Brush the chicken with safflower oil and season with salt and pepper. Grill the chicken on both sides, 5 to 7 minutes per side, or until the internal temperature reaches 165°F.

2. Put the spinach, cucumber ribbons, and shallot in a large bowl and toss with the dressing to combine well.

3. Divide the spinach mixture among four plates and top with the avocado slices, strawberries, walnuts, and grilled chicken. Serve immediately.

Variation Tip: If it's too late in the summer for fresh berries, seasonal stone fruit such as peaches and nectarines are also fabulous in this salad. Just pit them and cut into cubes.

Green Goddess Salad with Grilled Chicken

SERVES 4 / PREP TIME: 15 MINUTES
COOK TIME: 15 MINUTES

EQUIPMENT NEEDED: SPAGHETTI AND
RIBBON BLADES

By now I think that all of us know how good it is for us to include more dark, leafy greens in our diet. However, did you also know that your body needs a bit of fat to properly absorb the nutrients in the greens? This green goddess dressing, made with avocado, is one of my preferred ways to make sure you get all the benefits of eating your veggies! If you don't have a grill, you can cook the chicken in a skillet on the stove top. Follow the directions for cooking chicken breasts in Asian-Style Cobb Salad (page 100).

FOR THE DRESSING

1 avocado, pitted

2 tablespoons apple cider vinegar

⅓ cup plus 2 tablespoons water

¼ cup fresh Italian (flat-leaf) parsley

1 tablespoon freshly squeezed lemon juice

1 garlic clove, minced

10 fresh basil leaves

2 scallions, white and green parts

¼ teaspoon sea salt

1 tablespoon honey or maple syrup (optional)

FOR THE SALAD

1 pound boneless, skinless chicken breasts

1 tablespoon safflower oil

Sea salt

Freshly ground black pepper

8 cups baby spinach

¼ medium red onion, spiralized with the ribbon blade

1 medium red bell pepper, stemmed, spiralized with the ribbon blade, then seeded

1 medium carrot, spiralized with the spaghetti blade

2 cups cherry tomatoes

⅓ cup sliced almonds

Preheat the grill.

To make the dressing

Put all the ingredients for the dressing into a food processor or blender. Process until smooth and set aside.

To make the salad

1. Brush the chicken with the safflower oil and season with salt and pepper. Grill the chicken on both sides, 5 to 7 minutes per side, or until the internal temperature reaches 165°F.

2. Toss the spinach with the onion and bell pepper ribbons, carrot noodles, tomatoes, and almonds in a large bowl. Pour on the dressing and toss until well combined.

3. Divide the salad among four plates and top with the grilled chicken. Serve warm.

Tip: Not a fan of raw onions, even the sweet red ones? Spiralize a red onion, put it in a jar covered with a brine of half water and half apple cider vinegar, and marinate overnight in the refrigerator, for incredibly tangy and slightly sweet onions that are nothing like their raw counterparts.

Asian-Style Cobb Salad

EQUIPMENT NEEDED: SPAGHETTI AND
RIBBON BLADES

*I could probably live on Cobb salad for the rest
of my life if I had to, but sometimes you need a
bit more variety. This Cobb salad is a slight
twist on the original because it contains more
vegetables for crunch and color, along with an
Asian-style dressing for a pop of flavor.*

FOR THE DRESSING

2 tablespoons coconut aminos
2 tablespoons extra-virgin olive oil
2 tablespoons sesame oil
1 tablespoon apple cider vinegar
1 garlic clove, minced

FOR THE SALAD

1 tablespoon coconut oil
1 pound boneless, skinless chicken breasts
Sea salt
Freshly ground black pepper
1 head romaine lettuce, chopped
1 medium cucumber, spiralized with the
    spaghetti blade
1 medium carrot, peeled, spiralized with the
    spaghetti blade
¼ head red cabbage, spiralized with the ribbon blade
2 hardboiled eggs, diced
1 avocado, pitted and diced
4 scallions, white and green parts, sliced

To make the dressing

In a medium bowl, whisk together all the
ingredients for the dressing. Set aside.

To make the salad

1. Heat the coconut oil in a medium skillet
over medium heat. Season the chicken with
a pinch of salt and pepper. Place the chicken
breasts in the skillet and cook for 1 minute,
then flip and cover the pan with a tight-fitting
lid. Cook for 10 minutes, or until the internal
temperature reaches at least 165°F. Remove
the chicken breasts from the heat and let them
rest for 5 minutes, then slice the chicken.

2. While the chicken is cooking, mix the
romaine, cucumber and carrot noodles, and
cabbage ribbons in a large bowl. Toss with the
dressing until well combined.

3. Divide the lettuce and vegetable mixture
among four bowls and top with the sliced
chicken, eggs, avocado, and scallions.

Substitution Tip: Not a fan of chicken breasts
or simply prefer dark meat? You can also roast
a whole chicken (or use a rotisserie chicken) in place
of the chicken breasts.

Bread-Free BLT with Chipotle Ranch Dressing

EQUIPMENT NEEDED: RIBBON BLADE

There's nothing that will divide a crowd of health food enthusiasts like the topic of ranch dressing. Should kids be allowed to eat it? Does it teach kids (and adults for that matter) to eat their vegetables or teach them only to eat their vegetables when they're covered in ranch? Regardless of where you stand, this chipotle ranch is nothing like the one that comes in the bottle. Instead of being loaded with preservatives, vegetable oil, and sugar, this one uses raw cashews for a creamy base, along with spices, sea salt, and lime juice. If we're going to eat ranch, shouldn't it be made from real ingredients?

FOR THE DRESSING

½ cup raw cashews

⅓ cup plus 2 tablespoons water

2 tablespoons freshly squeezed lime juice

½ teaspoon garlic powder

½ teaspoon onion powder

½ teaspoon smoked paprika

½ teaspoon sea salt

¼ teaspoon chili powder

FOR THE SALAD

1 head romaine lettuce, chopped

1 green bell pepper, stemmed, spiralized with the ribbon blade, then seeded

1 medium cucumber, spiralized with the ribbon blade

¼ red onion, spiralized with the ribbon blade

4 strips nitrate-free bacon, cooked and chopped

2 cups cherry tomatoes, sliced

To make the dressing

Put all the ingredients for the dressing in a food processor or blender. Process until smooth. Set aside.

To make the salad

1. Mix the romaine, the bell pepper, cucumber ribbons, and red onion ribbons, and the bacon in a large bowl. Add the dressing and toss until well combined.

2. Divide the salad among four plates and top with the cherry tomatoes. Serve immediately.

Make It Vegan: Vegetarian or simply not a fan of bacon? Omit the bacon and add toasted nuts instead. This salad goes particularly well with lightly toasted almonds tossed with a touch of smoked paprika, chili powder, sea salt, and a squeeze of fresh lime juice.

Steak Salad with Romesco Sauce

SERVES 4 / PREP TIME: 20 MINUTES
COOK TIME: 20 MINUTES

EQUIPMENT NEEDED: RIBBON BLADE

If you've never had romesco sauce before, this is going to change your world. I first tried it over a steak salad, and have been so obsessed with this combination that I had to include a version of it here for you. If you have extra sauce left over, it can be kept in the fridge for up to seven days, and you will definitely want to put it on everything in sight: grilled vegetables, roasted chicken, zucchini pasta, and even omelets. I promise it won't disappoint.

1 red bell pepper, halved

2 cups cherry tomatoes, divided

2 tablespoons coconut oil, divided

4 (6-ounce) grass-fed sirloin steaks

⅓ cup raw almonds

1 tablespoon apple cider vinegar

1 garlic clove

1 teaspoon smoked paprika

½ teaspoon sea salt

1 tablespoon extra-virgin olive oil

2 medium summer squash, spiralized with the ribbon blade

6 cups baby arugula

Freshly ground black pepper

1. Preheat the broiler.

2. Line a baking sheet with aluminum foil and place the bell pepper and 1 cup of the cherry tomatoes on the baking sheet. Broil for 15 to 20 minutes, flipping as needed, until the bell pepper skin is blackened and the tomatoes are browned and softened.

3. Set the tomatoes aside. Place the pepper in a glass container with a tight-fitting lid for about 10 minutes, to allow the skin to steam and loosen.

4. When the pepper and tomatoes are about 10 minutes from being cooked, begin cooking the steaks. Heat 1 tablespoon of the coconut oil in a medium skillet over medium-high heat. Add the steaks and cook for 4 to 5 minutes per side, until the internal temperature reaches 145°F. Transfer to a plate to rest for 5 minutes, then thinly slice against the grain.

5. When the bell pepper has cooled and while the steak is resting, remove the skin with your fingers. If the skin is sticking to the pepper, a little bit of charred skin won't hurt. Remove the seeds and pith and add the pepper to a food processor or blender, along with the roasted tomatoes.

6. Add the almonds, vinegar, garlic, paprika, and salt to the blender. Process until smooth. If the mixture is too thick, add 1 or 2 tablespoons water, until the sauce reaches the desired consistency. Set aside.

7. Heat the remaining 1 tablespoon of coconut oil in the same skillet over medium heat. Add the squash ribbons and cook 2 to 3 minutes, until slightly tender but not mushy. Drain any liquid.

8. Divide the arugula among four plates. Top with the squash, reserved raw tomatoes, and sliced steak. Drizzle with the romesco sauce and season with black pepper.

Cooking Tip: If you have a gas stove, you can roast the pepper over the open flame instead of broiling it. Leave the bell pepper whole and, using a pair of tongs, set the pepper directly on the flame, turning until the skin is completely blackened. If you roast the bell pepper on the stove top, add the tomatoes to the sauce raw.

6

Hearty Soups

105

Ginger Egg Drop Soup

SERVES 2 TO 4 / PREP TIME: 5 MINUTES
COOK TIME: 5 MINUTES

EQUIPMENT NEEDED: SPAGHETTI BLADE

This simple soup is great for an easy side dish or a quick meal. I'll admit, I've been known to have this soup for breakfast. It's just that good.

4 cups vegetable broth
1-inch piece fresh ginger, grated
2 garlic cloves, minced
1 medium zucchini, spiralized with the spaghetti blade
2 medium eggs, beaten
1 tablespoon coconut aminos
1 teaspoon sesame oil
½ teaspoon sea salt
3 scallions, white and green parts, sliced
Freshly ground black pepper

1. In a medium pot, bring the broth, ginger, and garlic to a boil over high heat.

2. Add the zoodles and remove the pot from the heat.

3. Stirring the broth in a clockwise motion, slowly pour in the eggs to create egg ribbons.

4. Stir in the coconut aminos, sesame oil, salt, and scallions. Season with pepper and serve hot.

Cooking Tip: If you like your zoodles tender rather than al dente, let them boil for 1 minute before removing the pot from the heat.

Mushroom Ramen

VEGETARIAN

SERVES 2 / PREP TIME: 10 MINUTES
COOK TIME: 15 MINUTES

EQUIPMENT NEEDED: SPAGHETTI BLADE

This isn't an instant package of ramen, but it comes together almost as quickly. I love this dish as a simple lunch on a rainy weekend.

2 tablespoons coconut oil, divided
1 medium onion, sliced
1-inch piece ginger, grated
5 garlic cloves, minced
6 ounces shiitake mushrooms, sliced
4 cups vegetable broth
2 tablespoons coconut aminos
1 teaspoon sesame oil
2 medium zucchini, spiralized with the spaghetti blade
3 medium scallions, white and green parts, sliced
Sea salt
Freshly ground black pepper
4 eggs

1. Heat 1 tablespoon of the coconut oil in a medium pot over medium heat. Add the onion and sauté for 2 to 3 minutes. Add the ginger, garlic, and mushrooms, and sauté for 1 minute, until the ingredients are fragrant.

2. Add the broth and bring to a boil. Add the coconut aminos and sesame oil. Reduce the heat and simmer, covered, for 5 minutes, until the mushrooms are tender and the broth is rich.

3. Add the zoodles and let them cook for 1 to 2 minutes, then remove the pot from the heat. Stir in the scallions, and season with salt and pepper.

4. Heat the remaining 1 tablespoon of coconut oil in a skillet over medium heat. When the oil is shimmering, crack in the eggs, cover the skillet, and cook until the whites have set.

5. Serve the ramen in bowls, topped with the fried eggs.

Variation Tip: Craving a bit of heat? Add a sliced jalapeño pepper or a dash of red pepper flakes along with the scallions in step 3.

Anti-Inflammatory Udon Soup

SERVES 2 / PREP TIME: 10 MINUTES
COOK TIME: 15 MINUTES

EQUIPMENT NEEDED: FETTUCCINE BLADE

Udon are thick Japanese wheat noodles, traditionally served in a flavorful broth called dashi. This version combines the flavors of udon soup with anti-inflammatory foods such as mushrooms, turmeric, and fresh ginger. Since traditional dashi is a balance of savory and sweet, this broth uses fennel seeds, star anise, and cinnamon (instead of sugar) to balance out the saltiness of the broth.

4 cups vegetable broth
4 ounces shiitake mushrooms, sliced
1 cinnamon stick
1 whole star anise
1-inch piece ginger, grated
1 garlic clove, minced
3 tablespoons coconut aminos
1 teaspoon sea salt, plus more for final seasoning
½ teaspoon fennel seeds
¼ teaspoon ground turmeric
2 baby bok choy, thinly sliced
2 scallions, white and green parts, thinly sliced
2 medium summer squash, spiralized with the fettuccine blade
Freshly ground black pepper

1. Pour the broth into a medium pot and add the mushrooms, cinnamon stick, star anise, ginger, garlic, coconut aminos, salt, fennel seeds, and turmeric. Simmer for 10 minutes so the broth absorbs the flavors, then remove and discard the star anise and cinnamon stick.

2. Add the baby bok choy and simmer for 2 minutes. Add the scallions and squash noodles, and simmer for 3 to 4 minutes, or until the noodles are just tender.

3. Season with salt and pepper, and serve hot.

Variation Tip: To make this soup more filling, add a poached egg or a protein source of your choice while the noodles are simmering.

Spicy Kimchi Ramen

VEGAN

SERVES 2 / PREP TIME: 10 MINUTES
COOK TIME: 10 MINUTES

EQUIPMENT NEEDED: SPAGHETTI BLADE

Any of my friends will tell you that I am the most awkward dancer, but I make up for it by being a pretty decent cook (probably the only reason I am still invited to parties). Kimchi is definitely one of my specialties. But even better than a fresh batch of kimchi is a fresh batch of this spicy kimchi ramen.

1 tablespoon coconut oil
1 medium onion, sliced
1-inch piece ginger, grated
3 garlic cloves, minced
4 cups vegetable broth
2 baby bok choy, sliced
2 tablespoons coconut aminos
1 medium daikon radish, spiralized with the
  spaghetti blade
1 medium zucchini, spiralized with the spaghetti blade
3 medium scallions, white and green parts, sliced
½ cup kimchi (or as desired)
Sea salt

1. Heat the coconut oil in a medium pot over medium heat. Add the onion and sauté for 2 to 3 minutes. Add the ginger and garlic and cook for 1 minute, until fragrant.

2. Add the broth and bring to a boil. Add the bok choy, coconut aminos, daikon radish and zucchini noodles, and let them cook for 2 to 3 minutes, or until the vegetables reach the desired tenderness.

3. Remove the pot from the heat and add the scallions and kimchi.

4. Season with salt, and serve hot.

Ingredient Tip: To preserve the live probiotics in the kimchi, it should be added at the end and not directly heated. Also, some brands of kimchi contain fish sauce, so if this is a dietary concern, be sure to check the label—or make your own from scratch instead.

Jalapeño Veggie Noodle Soup

VEGAN

SERVES 4 / PREP TIME: 10 MINUTES
COOK TIME: 25 MINUTES

EQUIPMENT NEEDED: SPAGHETTI BLADE

When I was first learning how to cook, I began by teaching myself to make simple soups from scratch. For years, veggie soups were my go-tos, mostly because they are delicious, but also because they were one of the few things I knew how to make. Whether you're just learning to cook or are already a pro in the kitchen, try this soup; it is still one of my favorites.

1 tablespoon coconut oil

1 medium onion, chopped

4 garlic cloves, minced

4 celery stalks, diced

1 teaspoon ground cumin

1 teaspoon dried oregano

1 teaspoon sea salt, plus more for final seasoning

1 teaspoon dried thyme

4 cups vegetable broth

1 jalapeño pepper, sliced

1 large carrot, peeled, spiralized with the spaghetti blade

Freshly ground black pepper

Fresh cilantro, chopped, for garnish

1. Heat the coconut oil in a medium pot over medium heat. Add the onion, garlic, and celery, and cook for 5 minutes, until the onion is fragrant.

2. Add the cumin, oregano, salt, thyme, broth, and jalapeño pepper. Bring to a boil. Cover, reduce the heat, and simmer for 15 minutes, until the vegetables are just tender.

3. Add the carrot noodles and cook for 2 to 3 minutes, until the noodles are just tender.

4. Season with salt and pepper and garnish with fresh cilantro.

Ingredient Tip: If you're not a fan of spicy foods, seed the jalapeño pepper before adding it to the soup, or omit it entirely.

Cleansing Cabbage Stew

VEGAN

SERVES 4 / PREP TIME: 10 MINUTES
COOK TIME: 25 MINUTES

EQUIPMENT NEEDED: RIBBON BLADE

Before you get nervous and think I'm trying to talk you into some version of the cabbage soup diet, let me assure you that a) I'm definitely not, and b) this soup is actually good. This simple veggie soup is a great way to fill up before a light main course or to round out a meal.

1 tablespoon coconut oil
6 ounces cremini mushrooms, sliced
4 celery stalks, finely diced
2 medium carrots, finely diced
1 medium onion, finely diced
3 garlic cloves, minced
1 teaspoon dried basil
1 teaspoon dried oregano
1 teaspoon paprika
1 teaspoon sea salt, plus more for final seasoning
1 teaspoon dried thyme
4 cups vegetable broth
1 (28-ounce) can diced tomatoes
2 tablespoons tomato paste
½ small head green cabbage, spiralized with
   the ribbon blade
2 tablespoons apple cider vinegar
Freshly ground black pepper

1. Heat the coconut oil in a medium pot over medium heat. Add the mushrooms, celery, carrots, and onion, and cook for 5 minutes, until the onion is fragrant.

2. Add the garlic, basil, oregano, paprika, salt, thyme, broth, diced tomatoes with their juice, and tomato paste. Bring to a boil. Cover, reduce the heat, and simmer for 10 minutes, until the vegetables are just tender.

3. Add the cabbage ribbons and simmer for 10 minutes, until the cabbage ribbons are tender.

4. Add the vinegar. Season with salt and pepper and serve hot.

Variation Tip: To make this soup a one-pot meal, add a protein source such as ground beef, shredded chicken, or legumes for a vegan version.

Lemon and Chicken Soup

SERVES 4 / PREP TIME: 10 MINUTES
COOK TIME: 25 MINUTES

EQUIPMENT NEEDED: SPAGHETTI BLADE

When I think of summer soup, it's usually something cold like gazpacho or a chilled carrot soup. However, this Lemon and Chicken Soup is light, refreshing, and incredibly satisfying, especially on a summer evening. This pairs well with the Strawberry and Avocado Salad with Grilled Chicken (page 97) or the Zucchini Caprese (page 85) for a complete meal.

1 tablespoon coconut oil, divided
4 celery stalks, finely diced
3 garlic cloves, minced
2 medium carrots, finely diced
1 medium onion, finely diced
1 teaspoon ground cumin
1 teaspoon sea salt, plus more for final seasoning
1 teaspoon dried thyme
6 cups chicken or vegetable broth
2 cups cooked chicken, shredded
Zest and juice of 1 lemon
2 summer squash, spiralized with the spaghetti blade
Freshly ground black pepper

1. Heat the coconut oil in a medium pot over medium heat. Add the celery, garlic, carrots, and onion, and cook for 5 minutes, until the onion is fragrant.

2. Add the cumin, salt, thyme, and broth. Bring to a boil. Cover, reduce the heat, and simmer for 15 minutes, until the vegetables are just tender.

3. Add the shredded chicken, lemon zest, lemon juice, and summer squash noodles. Simmer for 1 to 3 minutes, or until the noodles are just tender.

4. Season with salt and pepper, and serve hot.

Cooking Tip: For a pretty presentation, float lemon slices on top of the soup.

Tom Kha Gai

SERVES 2 TO 4 / PREP TIME: 15 MINUTES
COOK TIME: 20 MINUTES

EQUIPMENT NEEDED: SPAGHETTI AND
RIBBON BLADES

I love the balance of spice and coconut milk in this soup. This is a great soup to make regardless of the weather, and I will often make the broth if I feel a cold coming on. Enjoy this as a main dish at dinner, or as a fabulous first course.

3 stalks fresh lemongrass

4 cups chicken or vegetable broth

Zest and juice of 1 lime

1-inch piece ginger, sliced

1 (13.5-ounce) can full-fat unsweetened coconut milk

4 ounces shiitake mushrooms, sliced

3 serrano chiles, sliced

2 cups shredded cooked chicken

2 cups chopped broccoli florets

1 medium onion, sliced

1 medium red bell pepper, stemmed, spiralized with the ribbon blade, then seeded

1 medium carrot, peeled, spiralized with the spaghetti blade

1 medium zucchini, spiralized with the spaghetti blade

Sea salt

⅓ cup chopped fresh cilantro

1. With the flat side of a large knife, pound and crush the lemongrass so it releases its flavor. Cut into 2-inch segments.

2. Pour the broth into a large pot over medium heat and bring to a boil. Add the lemongrass, lime zest, lime juice, and ginger. Reduce the heat and simmer, covered, for about 10 minutes.

3. Add the coconut milk, mushrooms, chiles, chicken, broccoli, onion, bell pepper ribbons, and carrot noodles, and simmer for 5 to 6 minutes, until the vegetables are just tender.

4. Add the zucchini and cook for 1 to 2 minutes, until the zoodles are just tender. Remove and discard the lemongrass and ginger slices.

5. Season with salt, garnish with the cilantro, and serve warm.

 Make It Vegan: Use vegetable broth and substitute sprouted tofu in place of the chicken.

Chicken Tortilla Soup

SERVES 4 / PREP TIME: 15 MINUTES
COOK TIME: 30 MINUTES

EQUIPMENT NEEDED: SPAGHETTI AND
RIBBON BLADES

If I could eat only one type of cuisine for the rest of my life, it would be a hard decision. But I know ultimately it would either be Asian or Mexican. This chicken tortilla soup is one of my favorites because it's hearty and filling without being unhealthy. And the best part: The spiralized carrots add a wonderful crunch that mimics the texture of the tortilla chips that would usually be on top!

2 tablespoons coconut oil, divided

1 pound boneless, skinless chicken breasts

½ teaspoon sea salt, plus a pinch

Freshly ground black pepper

2 garlic cloves, minced

1 jalapeño pepper, seeded and minced

1 medium onion, finely diced

1 teaspoon ground cumin

1 teaspoon smoked paprika

4 cups chicken broth

1 (14.5-ounce) can crushed tomatoes

2 tablespoons tomato paste

1 medium green bell pepper, stemmed, spiralized with the ribbon blade, then seeded

1 medium red bell pepper, stemmed, spiralized with the ribbon blade, then seeded

1 medium zucchini, spiralized with the spaghetti blade

1 medium carrot, peeled, spiralized with the spaghetti blade

1 avocado, pitted and sliced

¼ cup chopped fresh cilantro

1. Heat 1 tablespoon of the coconut oil in a medium skillet over medium heat. Season the chicken breasts with a pinch of salt and pepper and cook for 1 minute. Flip the chicken, cover the pan with a tight-fitting lid, and cook for 10 minutes, or until the internal temperature reaches at least 165°F. Remove from the heat and let them rest for 5 minutes, then slice or shred the chicken.

2. Add the remaining 1 tablespoon of coconut oil to a medium pot over medium heat. Add the garlic, jalapeño, onion, cumin, paprika, and ½ teaspoon of the salt. Sauté for 5 minutes, until the onion is translucent.

3. Add the broth, crushed tomatoes with their juice, tomato paste, and cooked chicken, and bring to a boil. Lower the heat and simmer, covered, for 10 minutes. Add the green and red bell pepper ribbons and zucchini noodles, and cook for 1 to 2 minutes, until the vegetables are just tender.

4. Divide between four bowls and top with the carrot noodles, avocado slices, and cilantro. Season with salt and pepper, and serve hot.

Ingredient Tip: Craving sour cream? Make your own dairy-free version by combining 1 cup of full-fat unsweetened coconut milk with 2 tablespoons of white vinegar. Mix well, then store in the refrigerator until you're ready to serve.

Classic Chicken Noodle Soup

SERVES 4 / PREP TIME: 10 MINUTES
COOK TIME: 30 MINUTES

EQUIPMENT NEEDED: SPAGHETTI BLADE

Is there anything more comforting than chicken noodle soup? This classic soup is a great dish to have in your repertoire. I usually double the recipe so I have enough leftovers for easy meals throughout the week.

2 tablespoons coconut oil, divided
1 pound boneless, skinless chicken thighs
3 medium carrots, peeled and chopped
3 medium celery stalks, chopped
3 garlic cloves, minced
1 medium onion, chopped
½ teaspoon sea salt, plus more for final seasoning
6 cups chicken broth
2 medium sweet potatoes, peeled, spiralized with the spaghetti blade
Freshly ground black pepper

1. Heat 1 tablespoon of the coconut oil in a medium skillet over medium heat. Add the chicken thighs in a single layer and cook for 3 to 5 minutes, until they are seared golden. Flip the thighs and cook the other side for 3 to 5 minutes, or until the chicken has reached an internal temperature of 165°F. Remove from the heat and shred.

2. Heat the remaining 1 tablespoon of coconut oil in a medium pot over medium heat. Add the carrots, celery, garlic, onion, and salt, and sauté for 5 minutes, or until the onion is translucent.

3. Add the chicken broth and shredded chicken. Bring to a boil, lower the heat, and simmer, covered, for 10 minutes. Add the sweet potato noodles and cook for 5 to 7 minutes, until the noodles are tender.

4. Season with sea salt and pepper, and serve hot.

Cooking Tip: Short on time? Reduce the cooking time by using shredded rotisserie chicken instead of cooking the chicken thighs from scratch.

Hearty Winter Pho

SERVES 2 / PREP TIME: 10 MINUTES
COOK TIME: 40 MINUTES

EQUIPMENT NEEDED: SPAGHETTI BLADE

Pho is a classic Vietnamese noodle soup. It's a staple in cold Seattle winters, and I couldn't survive a season without it. This version uses parsnip noodles to mimic the rice noodles in a traditional pho. Eat it curled up under a warm blanket and, preferably, while snuggling a cat.

1 cinnamon stick

1 whole star anise

2 large garlic cloves, sliced

2-inch piece ginger, peeled and roughly chopped

¼ medium onion, thinly sliced

4 cups chicken or vegetable broth

1 tablespoon coconut aminos

2 cups shredded cooked chicken

2 medium parsnips, peeled, spiralized with the spaghetti blade

1 lime, cut into wedges

2 large Thai basil sprigs

1 cup fresh mung bean sprouts

1 jalapeño pepper, sliced

1. In a large pot over medium heat, dry-roast the cinnamon stick, star anise, garlic, and ginger for 1 minute.

2. Add the onion, broth, and coconut aminos. Bring to a boil, reduce the heat, and simmer, covered, for 30 minutes. Remove and discard the cinnamon stick and star anise.

3. Add the chicken and the parsnip noodles. Simmer for 5 to 6 minutes, or until the noodles are tender but not mushy.

4. Serve hot with lime wedges, basil, bean sprouts, and jalapeño slices.

Variation Tip: I like to load up my pho with extra vegetables such as broccoli florets and baby bok choy. Also, if you're not a fan of parsnips, try substituting sweet potatoes, daikon radish, or celeriac in fall and winter, or carrots or zucchini in spring and summer.

Parsnip and Kale Zuppa Toscana

EQUIPMENT NEEDED: FETTUCCINE BLADE

Think coconut milk is only for curries or Asian cuisine? Think again. This recipe leaves out the heavy cream and white potatoes of a traditional Tuscan soup, and swaps in coconut milk, organic sausage, fresh kale, and spiralized parsnips. You won't even realize the cream is missing.

1 tablespoon coconut oil

1 pound ground Italian sausage, crumbled

1 medium onion, chopped

3 garlic cloves, minced

1 teaspoon dried basil

1 teaspoon dried oregano

½ teaspoon red pepper flakes

5 cups chicken or vegetable broth

½ cup full-fat unsweetened canned coconut milk

3 medium parsnips, peeled, spiralized with the fettuccine blade

1 bunch kale, torn into bite-size pieces

Sea salt

Freshly ground black pepper

1. Heat the coconut oil in a medium pot over medium heat. Add the sausage and cook until browned, about 5 minutes. Add the onion and cook for 5 minutes, until translucent.

2. Add the garlic, basil, oregano, red pepper flakes, and broth. Bring to a boil, lower the heat, and cover. Simmer for 20 minutes.

3. Add the coconut milk, parsnip noodles, and kale, and simmer, covered, for 5 to 6 minutes, or until the noodles and kale are just tender.

4. Season with salt and pepper, and serve hot.

Ingredient Tip: Look for sausage made from pork that is organic and pasture-raised, preferably purchased from a local farm. This ensures the animals received the best treatment and that there are no antibiotics or hormones in the meat. Veggie sausage can also be substituted, for a vegan option.

Weeknight Minestrone

SERVES 4 / PREP TIME: 10 MINUTES
COOK TIME: 40 MINUTES

EQUIPMENT NEEDED: FETTUCCINE BLADE

One of my traditional things to do in fall and winter is make a giant pot of soup on a Monday night, so I can use the leftovers as easy lunches for the rest of the week. This weeknight minestrone keeps well and develops even more flavor overnight. Serve it with a side salad for a complete meal.

1 tablespoon coconut oil

1 pound grass-fed ground beef

3 medium carrots, finely diced

3 celery stalks, finely diced

3 garlic cloves, minced

1 medium onion, finely diced

1 teaspoon dried basil

1 teaspoon dried oregano

½ teaspoon sea salt, plus more for final seasoning

2 bay leaves

1 (28-ounce) can diced tomatoes

2 tablespoons tomato paste

2 cups vegetable broth

2 medium zucchini, spiralized with the fettuccine blade

Freshly ground black pepper

1. Heat the coconut oil in a large pot over medium heat. Add the ground beef. Cook, stirring frequently, for 10 minutes, until the beef is well browned. Drain any excess fat from the pot.

2. Add the carrots, celery, garlic, onion, basil, oregano, and salt. Cook, stirring frequently, for 5 minutes, until the onion is tender and the spices are fragrant.

3. Add the bay leaves, diced tomatoes with their juice, tomato paste, and broth. Increase the heat and bring to a boil, reduce the heat to a simmer, and cook, covered, for about 20 minutes, or until the vegetables are tender.

4. Add the zucchini noodles and cook for 2 to 3 minutes, until the zoodles are just tender.

5. Remove and discard the bay leaves. Season with salt and pepper, and serve hot.

Make It Vegan: Omit the ground beef and substitute one (15-ounce) can of kidney beans, drained and well rinsed. Add the beans to the pot along with the broth in step 3.

Slow Cooker Thai Beef Soup

SERVES 4 / PREP TIME: 15 MINUTES
COOK TIME: 8 HOURS

EQUIPMENT NEEDED: SPAGHETTI BLADE

If you work outside your home full-time, like I do, or just have a busy schedule, I'm sure you appreciate a good slow cooker recipe. I usually end up making some variation of this soup once a month during the winter. It's also a wonderful and simple main dish for entertaining.

1 tablespoon coconut oil

1 pound grass-fed boneless beef chuck roast, trimmed of excess fat

4 tablespoons Thai red curry paste

4 garlic cloves, minced

1 medium onion, sliced

1 teaspoon sea salt, plus more for final seasoning

6 cups beef broth

2 tablespoons coconut aminos

2 stalks fresh lemongrass, sliced

2 medium daikon radishes, peeled, spiralized with the spaghetti blade

2 teaspoons lime zest

Freshly ground black pepper

½ cup fresh Thai basil leaves

3 scallions, white and green parts, sliced

1. Heat the coconut oil in a medium skillet over medium-high heat. Add the chuck roast and sear for 1 to 2 minutes, turn, and sear the other side. Place the chuck roast in the slow cooker.

2. Add the curry paste, garlic, and onion to the same skillet and cook, stirring frequently, for about 30 seconds, until fragrant. Add the mixture to the slow cooker, along with the salt, broth, coconut aminos, and lemongrass.

3. Cook on low for 6 to 8 hours, or until the beef is tender.

4. Turn the slow cooker to high, add the daikon radish noodles and lime zest, and simmer for 5 to 6 minutes, or until the noodles are tender.

5. Season with salt and pepper, and top with the basil leaves and scallions. Serve hot.

Cooking Tip: Searing the meat and quickly browning the garlic and onion adds depth and flavor to the soup. However, if you are short on time, you can skip these steps and add all the ingredients directly to the slow cooker.

Beefy Tomato Soup

SERVES 4 / PREP TIME: 10 MINUTES
COOK TIME: 35 MINUTES

EQUIPMENT NEEDED: FETTUCCINE BLADE

If you're a fan of a classic creamy tomato soup, you're going to love this! This hearty (but low-carb) recipe gets its creaminess by blending cashews with the broth for a rich, dairy-free soup. It's the perfect quick one-pot weeknight meal, or an easy soup to serve to guests at a dinner party.

1 tablespoon coconut oil

1 pound grass-fed ground beef

3 garlic cloves, chopped

1 medium onion, chopped

1 teaspoon dried basil

1 teaspoon ground cumin

1 teaspoon dried oregano

1 teaspoon sea salt, plus more for final seasoning

1 teaspoon dried thyme

1 (28-ounce) can diced tomatoes

4 tablespoons tomato paste

3 cups vegetable or beef broth, divided

⅓ cup raw cashews

2 medium zucchini, spiralized with the fettuccine blade

Freshly ground black pepper

1. Heat the coconut oil in a large pot over medium heat. Add the ground beef. Cook, stirring frequently, for 10 minutes, until the beef is well browned. Drain any excess fat from the pot and add the garlic, onion, basil, cumin, oregano, salt, and thyme. Cook, stirring frequently, for 5 minutes, until the onion is tender and the spices are fragrant.

2. Add the diced tomatoes and their juice, tomato paste, and 2 cups of the broth. Bring to a boil, lower the heat to a simmer, and cook for 15 minutes, stirring occasionally.

3. While the soup is simmering, put the remaining 1 cup of broth in the blender with the cashews and process until smooth.

4. Add the cashew broth and zoodles to the soup. Cook for 2 to 3 minutes, or until the vegetables are tender.

5. Season with salt and pepper, and serve hot.

Variation Tip: For a leaner soup, you can substitute turkey instead of the beef. You can also make the soup vegetarian or vegan by using vegetable broth and a protein source of your choice.

Appendix A

Measurement Conversions

VOLUME EQUIVALENTS (DRY)

US STANDARD	METRIC (APPROXIMATE)
⅛ teaspoon	0.5 mL
¼ teaspoon	1 mL
½ teaspoon	2 mL
¾ teaspoon	4 mL
1 teaspoon	5 mL
1 tablespoon	15 mL
¼ cup	59 mL
⅓ cup	79 mL
½ cup	118 mL
⅔ cup	156 mL
¾ cup	177 mL
1 cup	235 mL
2 cups or 1 pint	475 mL
3 cups	700 mL
4 cups or 1 quart	1 L
½ gallon	2 L
1 gallon	4 L

VOLUME EQUIVALENTS (LIQUID)

US STANDARD	US STANDARD (OUNCES)	METRIC (APPROXIMATE)
2 tablespoons	1 fl. oz.	30 mL
¼ cup	2 fl. oz.	60 mL
½ cup	4 fl. oz.	120 mL
1 cup	8 fl. oz.	240 mL
1½ cups	12 fl. oz.	355 mL
2 cups or 1 pint	16 fl. oz.	475 mL
4 cups or 1 quart	32 fl. oz.	1 L
1 gallon	128 fl. oz.	4 L

OVEN TEMPERATURES

FAHRENHEIT (F)	CELSIUS (C) (APPROXIMATE)
250°F	120°C
300°F	150°C
325°F	165°C
350°F	180°C
375°F	190°C
400°F	200°C
425°F	220°C
450°F	230°C

WEIGHT EQUIVALENTS

US STANDARD	METRIC (APPROXIMATE)
½ ounce	15 g
1 ounce	30 g
2 ounces	60 g
4 ounces	115 g
8 ounces	225 g
12 ounces	340 g
16 ounces or 1 pound	455 g

The Dirty Dozen & Clean Fifteen

A nonprofit and environmental watchdog organization called Environmental Working Group (EWG) looks at data supplied by the US Department of Agriculture (USDA) and the Food and Drug Administration (FDA) about pesticide residues and compiles a list each year of the best and worst pesticide loads found in commercial crops. You can refer to the Dirty Dozen list to know which fruits and vegetables you should always buy organic. The Clean Fifteen list lets you know which produce is considered safe enough when grown conventionally to allow you to skip the organics. This does not mean that the Clean Fifteen produce is pesticide-free, though, so wash these fruits and vegetables thoroughly.

These lists change every year, so make sure you look up the most recent before you fill your shopping cart. You'll find the most recent lists as well as a guide to pesticides in produce at EWG.ORG/FOODNEWS.

2016 DIRTY DOZEN

Apples	Snap peas	*In addition to the Dirty Dozen, the EWG added two foods contaminated with highly toxic organo-phosphate insecticides:*
Celery	Spinach	
Cherry tomatoes	Strawberries	
Cucumbers	Sweet bell peppers	
Grapes		
Nectarines		Hot peppers
Peaches		Kale/Collard greens
Potatoes		

2016 CLEAN FIFTEEN

Asparagus	Mangos
Avocados	Onions
Cabbage	Papayas
Cantaloupe	Pineapples
Cauliflower	Sweet corn
Eggplant	Sweet peas (frozen)
Grapefruit	
Kiwis	Sweet potatoes

Resources

Becky Selengut

www.beckyselengut.com
Becky is a chef, instructor, and author with whom I've worked for years. If you want to learn more about basic cooking techniques, or specific techniques related to cooking with mushrooms or seafood, Becky's website is the best resource around.

Center for Urban Education about Sustainable Agriculture

www.cuesa.org/eat-seasonally/charts/vegetables
Curious about what produce is in season when? Check out CUESA's website for a handy seasonal produce chart.

Environmental Working Group

www.ewg.org
Looking for more resources about eating organic? Each year, the Environmental Working Group tests the pesticide residue in different produce and updates their Dirty Dozen list (produce with the most pesticide residue) and their Clean Fifteen list (produce with the least pesticide residue). Check out their website for more information.

In Sonnet's Kitchen

www.insonnetskitchen.com
Love the recipes in this book? Check out my blog, *In Sonnet's Kitchen*, for more seasonal recipes and healthy cooking tips.

Inspiralized

inspiralized.com
Inspiralized was founded by Ali Maffucci in 2013 to share her love of spiralizing and cooking, and it's been incredible to watch her blog and brand grow over the years. Ali is the queen of everything spiralized, so check out her website for great recipes and videos.

Monterey Bay Aquarium Seafood Watch

www.montereybayaquarium.org/ conservation-and-science/our-programs/ seafood-watch
The Monterey Bay Aquarium's Seafood Watch program is the best resource to help consumers choose sustainable seafood. Visit their website for more information about the best choices for your area.

Non-GMO Project

www.nongmoproject.org
Stay up-to-date on the latest news about genetically modified organisms and get involved to protect the availability of non-GMO foods.

Looking for more food blogs? Some of my favorites include

* Danielle Walker's Against All Grain, *againstallgrain.com*

* Diane Sanfilippo's Balanced Bites, *balancedbites.com*

* Green Kitchen Stories, *www.greenkitchenstories.com*

* Minimalist Baker, *minimalistbaker.com/recipes/*

* My New Roots, *www.mynewroots.org/site/*

* Pinch of Yum, *pinchofyum.com*

* Sarah Wilson, *www.sarahwilson.com*

* Sprouted Kitchen, *www.sproutedkitchen.com*

* Wellness Mama, *wellnessmama.com*

Recipe Index

Index

Acknowledgments

I could not have done this book without the love and support of many people in my life.

First off, thank you to every chef and cooking instructor I have ever worked with. I've learned so much from each and every one of you (too many of you to name!), and each of those lessons will never be forgotten. Some of my favorite memories are of the long hours I've spent in hot kitchens around Seattle, and I'm so grateful for all of those experiences and how they have influenced my cooking today.

Every person who works with food knows that the quality of the ingredients matters. After all, every recipe tastes better when you start with fresh, seasonal, and local ingredients. I'm grateful to each farmer and every hand involved in producing the food I eat before it comes to my table.

Thank you to all my blog readers, social media followers, newsletter subscribers, and you, dear reader, for purchasing this cookbook. When I began my food blog, *In Sonnet's Kitchen*, in 2010, I had no idea what it would grow into, and I'm grateful each and every day to be able to share my recipes and creations with you. After all, without my blog, I would probably just be the crazy lady in her kitchen talking to her cats.

To my friends, all of you: thank you, thank you, thank you! I can't tell you how much you mean to me, but I'm avoiding listing specific names because I think it might make me cry. (And since I'm currently writing this in a crowded Seattle coffee shop, crying in public might not be the best idea.) I'm so fortunate to be surrounded by such a loving, supportive community of people and, hopefully, I will see you again soon now that this book is finished.

To my wonderful partner, thank you for the many, many loads of dishes you handwashed, the hours you spent cleaning up the kitchen after me, and for always making me laugh when I was in the midst of a meltdown spurred by a recipe failure. There's no way I could have done this without you, and I'm so lucky to have you by my side.

To my mother and brother, thank you for your constant support and encouragement, especially when I needed it the most. You have always been a rock in my life and I'm grateful to the both of you for putting up with me.

To my cats Bilbo and Frodo, thank you for keeping me up at night, running through the kitchen while I'm trying to cook, and lying across my keyboard each time I sit down to write a recipe. This experience wouldn't have been the same without you.

About the Author

SONNET LAUBERTH, MA, is a Certified Holistic Health Coach, food blogger, freelance recipe developer, writer, and cookbook author. She has been writing her blog, *In Sonnet's Kitchen*, since 2010, and is passionate about simple, healthy cooking; supporting local farmers; and eating with the seasons. When she's not cooking or writing, she can be found swinging kettlebells, doing yoga, reading at the beach, or listening to bad '90s music. She lives in Seattle, Washington, with her partner and two cats.